I0816688

"For decades as both poet and proser, Chris Wiman has infected nonbelievers and believers alike with books that mesmerize with both salvation and catastrophe. So I devoured *Glimmerings*—a marvel of discourse between him and theologian Miroslav Volf—in one sitting: beautiful & wise, provocative, bold, and haunting. It's destined to become a classic. Buy this book!"

— Mary Karr, *New York Times* bestselling author of
The Liar's Club, *Cherry*, and *Lit*

"Here are two exceptionally intelligent, imaginative people, pushing, challenging, deeply appreciating and supporting one another, as together they think through the sheer strangeness of belief. A profoundly honest, moving conversation that will prompt the reader again and again to want to join in."

— Rowan Williams, theologian, poet, and former
archbishop of Canterbury

"Reading these letters, you know you are in the hands of craftsmen of language who use that language to explore questions of God, mortality, fear, limitations, regrets and ambitions.

Theirs is a friendship electrified by intellect and fruitful divergence. Where they differ, they engage, reflect and ask more. These letters are an intimate glimpse into lives caught up in a brotherhood of exploration."

— Pádraig Ó Tuama, Irish poet and theologian

"Reading the letters between two of the finest minds and souls of our times—Volf, a renowned theologian, and Wiman, an inscriptional poet—feels like curling up in front of a fire, unseen, to half-overhear and half-understand two contemporary ancients groping toward meaning. In the profound friendship so alive in these tender epistles, a poet and a theologian wrestle with their distinct understandings of God, faith, and faith's absence. *Glimmerings* is an act of devotion and of divine consciousness at play."

— Eliza Griswold, Pulitzer Prize–winning journalist
and author of *Circle of Hope*

"Arresting in beauty and remarkable in its all-too-rare honesty, *Glimmerings* is a gem of a book I will be returning to time and again . . . This is a deeply Christian book yet, as a non-Christian,

I was able to find both challenge and inspiration on almost every page. What a beautiful book this is."

— Shai Held, President of the Hadar Institute and author of *Judaism Is About Love: Recovering the Heart of Jewish Life*

"'We are trying,' writes one of the authors of this remarkable exchange, 'trying to understand each other—to articulate and make plausible . . . our experience with God, Christ, faith, and the lack of it.' What results, wondrous to behold, is lived theology in the making . . . Probing intelligence, rhetorical eloquence, passages of extraordinary self-disclosure, expressions of affection. I know of nothing like it. Take, read, and savor."

— Nicholas Wolterstorff, Noah Porter Professor Emeritus of Philosophical Theology, Yale University

GLIMMERINGS

GLIMMERINGS

Letters on Faith Between a Poet and a Theologian

MIROSLAV VOLF AND
CHRISTIAN WIMAN

HARPERONE
An Imprint of HarperCollins*Publishers*

The permissions on page 253 constitute a continuation of this copyright page.

HarperCollins books may be purchased for educational, business, or sales promotional use. For information, please email the Special Markets Department at SPsales@harpercollins.com.

harpercollins.com

FIRST EDITION

Designed by Jason Kayser

Library of Congress Cataloging-in-Publication Data has been applied for.

ISBN 978-0-06-345829-1

25 26 27 28 29 LBC 5 4 3 2 1

IN MEMORIAM

Jürgen Moltmann (1926–2024)

Fanny Howe (1940–2025)

Glimmerings are what the soul's composed of.

—SEAMUS HEANEY

CONTENTS

PREFACE

The sociologists tell us that women prefer conversing eye to eye while men do better with some degree of peripheral attention, at least when talking with other men. True or not, for years the two of us have taken walks together, setting out from the divinity school where we both teach and making the same regular loop through the streets of New Haven. After catching up on our respective lives and loves, our talk inevitably turns to some issue of theology, philosophy, or literature one of us is wrestling with. We don't solve any of the old conundrums, but then that's not really the point. The point is to nourish a friendship that has changed and sustained both of us. Occasionally, though, because one of us is sick or one is traveling, or for a semester our schedules are simply too mismatched, we fall out of touch for a while. It was during one of these times that a brief email exchange sparked a question—*the* question—at the heart of Christianity, as well as many other religions: What does it mean to love God? It was Jesus's chief injunction, of course, though he was getting it from the Hebrew scriptures. That spark flared, and after a frenetic (and pretty messy) series of emails, we realized we'd struck something deep in both of us, and also that we'd found a way to walk, so to speak, when we couldn't. That first question is not how this book begins, but it's fair to say that the entire exchange is a response to it.

MV and CW

FEBRUARY 28

Dear Miroslav,

I don't know what faith means anymore. I'm fifty-six years old with a pile of books behind me and an experimental bone marrow transplant ahead of me, and I don't know what faith means.

But that's just the beginning of the problem. Do you know that scene in Joyce's *Ulysses* with Stephen Dedalus: "I fear those big words, Stephen said, which make us so unhappy"? I forget the exact words he's referring to—history, I think, is the main one. It's the idea of the encompassing abstraction that appalls him. I sometimes think that's where I am with regard to Christianity. I fear those big words—faith, grace, sin, redemption, love—which make us so sad.

Why sad? Because they seethe and shift and slip free from meaning. Because they seem to demand some whole-souled attention but are not stable enough to warrant that. Because they are both necessary and impossible, and pinch individual life in that vise.

I know from our many walks and talks over the years that

this is not exactly the case for you, but do you feel this linguistic/existential problem that I do? Or perhaps to be more specific: How would you define faith at this point in your life? Not before God but before humans—in an email, say?

Chris

MARCH 5

Dear Chris,

When you listed your own "big words which make us so sad," my mind went to Moses's encounter with God in the burning bush. Speaking from the restless flame, God says to Moses, "I have observed the misery of my people who are in Egypt; I have heard their cry on account of their taskmasters. Indeed, I know their sufferings, and I have come down to deliver them from the Egyptians, and to bring them up out of that land to a good and broad land . . ." I grew up with a different set of big words, proclaimed with finger-wagging and fist-slamming by semidictatorial rulers. Some ten years before I was born, in what was at the time Yugoslavia, words like "revolution," "proletariat," and "brotherhood and unity" sent my then-teenage father on a death march. I, too, felt their force beating me, even as a nine-year-old, into wishing, at times, my nonexistence for being the son of a minister. For me, big and semantically unstable Christian words mostly became "good and broad land," hospitable spaces in which I could live without pressure, face unconquered giants, and occasionally feast on the promised milk and honey. I don't know whether you have had a chance to look at Moltmann's autobiography, which is about his coming to faith and his lifelong wrestling with it. It is titled *A Broad Place*. I resonate with the title. He, too, almost perished by big words, though National-Socialist ones rather than Leninist ones like my father.

What sometimes assails me, a giant that I cannot but let be, is not so much the instability of "faith" as it is the experience of its content just vanishing, which may be what you mean by big words slipping "free from meaning." In the space where God was present to me, there is—nothing. My life continues in its inertias, but at the edge of my experiences, I sense a cosmic motherlessness: I am in my little boat on the open seas with no land in sight. When the seas are calm, things seem bereft of meaning; when the seas rage, terror is on all sides. I am channeling Nietzsche here, a section from his *The Joyful Science* just before the famous passage about the madman and the death of God (Nietzsche borrowed the metaphor from Schopenhauer and, like much he borrowed, used it in his own way). Nietzsche's way of seeing the world is my temptation, as I am sure I've told you.

As I have aged, I have come to believe that my faith matters much less than I thought it did when I was younger. I am saved by God's faithfulness, not primarily by my faith. My faith is a fruit of God's faithfulness, not the condition of God's arrival into my soul—and into my speech. I have always had as much faith as was needed to say, *if* there is God, then nothing can separate me from God's love—not the instability inside the abstraction that faith might be, not even utter lack of faith. I don't trust in my faith. Nor my love. Even at my best, I am incapable of the "whole-souled attention" that God actually commands. (What a wonderful rendering of the first commandment!) When my faith becomes empty, I wait for God to return into my faith, to dock my little boat on the shore. Faith is not a way to hold God close. Faith is trust that God will see me, hear me, know me . . . and come.

"God" is the biggest of the big words and a very unstable linguistic space. Sometimes, for no apparent reason, it suddenly empties itself of meaning for me, most often, for some reason, in the middle of a prayer. But when it doesn't, that word moves me and makes me quietly rejoice. Not the word "God" as such, but God's cryptic self-description to Moses, which follows upon the promise of exodus. When I "hear" God say, "I am who I am," I gloss it with "and I will remain that always, also for you." I then become one of the children of Israel. I feel myself taken out of my own narrowness, out of the dominion of some little Pharaoh, and transported into the wideness of God's self-commitment to me—and to the whole world. I always think of "God," a word whose meaning shifts more than the restless flame from which God spoke to Moses, as a *promise*. Sometimes I also experience it as such.

Miroslav

MARCH 10

Dear Miroslav,

I find it very consoling to think of my faith not mattering so much, of it being mostly a form of patience. I'm always quoting to my students Barth's statement that faith is not an *achievement*, but I live with a kind of restless and appetitive drive that often seems to belie that. The thing is, I can't help but see this hunger as a "gift" from God. All of my writing has come out of it, every word, even in works that seem to have nothing to do with God. I am *after* something, and that something is also after me. Sometimes we meet—vision? collision? it's hard to say—and our lives catalyze each other and are one force, one love. So maybe, in terms of faith, there is a good hunger and a bad hunger. The former lives with no expectation of permanent fulfillment. "Glimmerings are what the soul's composed of," as Seamus Heaney puts it in "Old Pewter." One gathers one's soul, one's god, fitfully, fugitively, and is content with that. Though everything I have written so far—and not just in these emails but literally *everything I have written so far*—suggests I am a long way from being content with that. Bad hunger.

The word "catalyze" in the paragraph above suggests a different conception of God between us. I don't think God is this entity out there altogether apart from us. "The eye with which I see God is the eye with which God sees me," says Meister Eckhart, a quote which I'm sure you know and which is no doubt overused. But it does get at an important truth. Attention enables God's presence. The life and love that are God are catalyzed by the life and love we expend in his direction, whatever form that expenditure takes (art, prayer, worship, theology, maybe *anything* beneficent that is done with "absolutely unmixed attention," as Weil puts it). God really is more of a verb than a noun, as are our "selves."

Given all this, it matters enormously what words we use to seek God. At least for some of us. I don't find those "big words" broad and spacious places. I find them fuzzy and gauzy and obscuring of the very thing they are meant to illuminate. You mention that Moltmann book. Of course, I read it when it came out because, as you know, Moltmann's *The Crucified God* is a book of immense and durable importance to me. But I wasn't able to finish the memoir. It seemed to me deadened by a kind of newspaper prose, no sense of pacing or structure or any of the elements that make that kind of writing come alive.

Technique is the test of an artist's sincerity, says Ezra Pound. There are ethical consequences to technical decisions. Pound is talking about art (certainly memoir is a form of art), but life, too, is a kind of art, and there are spiritual ramifications to the linguistic decisions/efforts/failures we make therein.

God as promise, as you put it? Yes, definitely, another consoling notion. But that seems to me a goad to an ever-further refinement of our forms of faith. You say you don't trust your own faith. I guess I don't either, except in the making of art, when trusting in my own faith (in poetry? in life and love? in God? I'm not sure it matters) is the only way that true art gets made. I hope I'm also trusting in God's promise in these moments. I certainly have experienced many moments when my own faith seems to be answered—or, maybe more accurately, fulfilled, a moment of being so replete and consummate that the word "faith" just falls away. How to make a life out of these moments? How to turn this mystical sense of God into a daily faith? How to simply *rest* in God? These are questions I still struggle to answer.

Chris

MARCH 16

Dear Chris,

Unlike you, I don't have the kind of intense hunger for God that animates my entire life. If I were to express my experience of God spatially, I would say that I sense God more behind and underneath me, but that somehow the space above me and in front of me into which I would stretch feels void of God. I am less reaching for God than recognizing, at times, that God is holding me. I have a deep sense of gratitude and awe for God's love, but not thirst and hunger. Sometimes I think that's because I don't quite know where to direct that thirst and hunger. But that cannot be right, because I seem to know where to direct gratitude and awe, or at least I act *as if* I know.

I don't think whether one hungers for God or not has much to do with our different understandings of God. I need to hear more, though, about how you think of the relation between God and the world. From what I can discern now, I don't think the difference is that I think that God is an entity out there whereas you don't. I do distinguish rather sharply between

God and the world, but I don't separate the two. I do believe, though, that I must be able to *think* God without the world, as you put it, "altogether apart from us." In the beginning, there was God and nothing but God: "The Word was with God, and the Word was God," as the prologue to John puts it. And then—in a kind of unthinkable atemporal sequence—God made "all things." I take this to mean that God isn't a thing, or at least that God isn't the kind of thing as are all the things that God has made and keeps in existence. Denys Turner, who was still teaching, I think, when you came to Yale, used to say when explaining what it means to say that God is not a thing: "Suppose, in the conduct of some quite lunatic thought-experiment, you were to imagine counting the total number of things that there are, have ever been, and will ever be, and you get to the number *n*. Then I say: 'Fine, that's the universe enumerated, but you have left out just one being, the being who made all that vast number of things that is the universe, namely God,' and, because you are not an atheist, you agree that this is so. Do you now add God to the list? Does the total number of things that there are now amount to $n+1$?" The answer is no, because "God's oneness is not such that God is one *more* in any numerable series whatever." I am not sure I entirely agree with Denys, but he is onto something important. Still, whatever kind of entity distinct from the world God is, God isn't only "out there." God is also here, closer to you and me than we are to ourselves. God is in our souls, behind our wills. God is the life of the world's liveliness.

You rightly suspected that I would object to your use of "catalyzing." As I see it, nothing creatures do can catalyze the "life and love that are God." I take it to be a metaphysical impossibility for humans to "catalyze" God. But perhaps with God's "life and love" you refer to no more than a certain form of *God's agency in the world*: beneficent acts done with "absolutely unmixed attention" mediating God's presence and activity in the world. As I was writing the second part of the last sentence, I found myself letting out a big sigh. The "absolute unmixed attention" both you and Weil seem to expect I cannot deliver. She might as well ask me to turn myself into an angel. To live is to be unjust, claimed Nietzsche. I agree, and I suspect that this applies to Saint Francis and not just to sinner Miroslav. I have a deep sense that all my motives, goals, and strivings—anything I do and am—are always and incorrigibly *also* nonbeneficent, always partly harming both others and my own self. God is unmixed love; God has no interest of God's own that God pursues in any way at the expense of any creature. In contrast, I always catalyze good and bad, beauty and ugliness, justice and injustice—so much so that it is not clear to me where exactly one ends and the other begins. The world and I myself need to be redeemed—from me. I am always also the problem with the world, even if it may be true that I am also part of the solution. No act of my own left to itself is in intention and effects only good; each is a line that needs straightening and redirecting. My love can be love only to the extent that it participates in God's love, or, rather, to the extent that God is doing the loving through me. God catalyzes me and my love; I don't catalyze either God or God's love in the world. Though I can be its instrument.

In relation to God, trust is for me more basic than appetitive, unitive love. That's because I don't think that union with God is dependent on my hunger for God, not even on my hunger construed as a divine gift. Union is itself a gift given in the gift of faith. On my good days I seek to open myself to God's love. The best I can do right now is to seek to love the Love that God is, to love what God loves and how God loves, to strive to open myself to become God's channel. Perhaps this is my kind of hunger and thirst for God, for God's righteousness.

Still, I know that I *should* love God directly. That's what Martin Luther, to whom I owe most of what I wrote above, insisted on. God's love for me should generate my love for God: "The heart overflows with gladness and goes leaping and dancing for the great pleasure it has found in God," Luther writes in his commentary on the Magnificat. I don't recall having ever leapt and danced out of love for God. And even if I had, that wouldn't have been enough. Luther thinks that God's love for me should generate a completely disinterested love for God, which is God's kind of love. I should love God not only for being good to me; I should also love "the bare, unfelt goodness that is hidden in God." If I could love and trust the bare goodness of God, I would be free no matter what happened in my life. I need such love for God now, urgently, but I suspect that I'll have it only in the world to come. Your own "expectation of permanent fulfillment," the stilling of hunger, is perhaps also an eschatological hope. Not bad hunger, but good hunger that cannot yet be satisfied.

This letter has grown too long, and I have not yet returned

to the important topic of language about God, which you raised in your first letter and then again in the second. I will return to it, including to your comments about Moltmann, in one of my next letters.

Miroslav

PS. It seems strange writing this email while you are receiving a bone marrow transplant and putting final touches on it while not knowing how the surgery went. But our love for God and God's love for us has everything to do with both our strength and our utter fragility.

MARCH 20

Dear Miroslav,

I really threw us off course with that word "beneficent." I simply meant to exclude certain malign forms of attention. A torturer, for instance, is presumably paying very close attention to his work, though that's obviously not the kind of attention Weil means to celebrate.

I take your point about all of our actions being inevitably compromised by our natures, but surely you have known those moments of attention when time vanishes and the soul is set free. I live for these moments in writing, but if I am honest, I have *never* known such a moment in prayer. This makes me sad and perhaps less critical of Weil than I should be.

To think God without the world? Nope, *that* seems to me a metaphysical impossibility. This is what I mean about the fallacy of thinking of God as "out there," as having some sort of independent existence from us. God is relation, full stop. He is like reality in this regard. Consider an electron, the fundamental unit of all matter. No one has ever seen one. They really don't "exist" until we turn our attention to them. The physicist Marcelo Gleiser says that "exist" may be too strong a word to use for an electron. I take

God's existence to be much the same, though for God "exist" is too weak a word. We don't know what the existence of God is. We have no idea what the word "exist" even means in the context of God. What we do know—or what I know, I should say—is that God doesn't exist until I turn my attention to him. Relation brings him into being, or, more accurately, enables his being to be perceived, experienced, shared. My attention—and the precise quality of that attention—is absolutely involved. I realize this is unorthodox at best, heretical at worst. But it is my experience of being in the world and of being with God. "The feeling remains," as Teresa of Avila says, "that God is on the journey, too."

That should go some way toward answering your question of how I conceive of God's relation to the world. God seems to *need* us, which again is far from the orthodox conception of God. I like this stanza from Robert Browning's poem "Rabbi Ben Ezra":

> But I need, now as then,
> Thee, God, who mouldest men;
> And since, not even while the whirl was worst,
> Did I,—to the wheel of life
> With shapes and colours rife,
> Bound dizzily,—mistake my end, to slake Thy thirst.

So the hunger I have described is a reciprocal one, and the goal of a good life is to satisfy the hunger that God has for us. *God in Search of Man* is my favorite book by Abraham Joshua Heschel, not simply because it beautifully articulates the divine hunger I am describing, but because it preserves a sense of God as utterly beyond. To conceive of God without the world and without human perceptions is not only impossible but, in much theology, actively destructive. Here's how Heschel puts it:

> One of the fatal errors of conceptual theology has been the separation of the acts of religious existence from the statements about it. Ideas of faith must not be studied in total separation from the moments of faith. If a plant is uprooted from its soil, removed from its native winds, sun-rays and terrestrial environment, and kept in a hothouse—will observations made of such a plant disclose its primordial nature? The growing inwardness of man that reaches and curves toward the light of God can hardly be transplanted into the shallowness of mere reflection. Torn out of its medium in human life, it wilts like a rose pressed between the pages of a book. Religion is, indeed, little more than a desiccated remnant of

> a once living reality when reduced to terms and definitions, to codes and catechisms. It can only be studied in its natural habitat of faith and piety, in a soul where the divine is within reach of all thoughts.

But all of this is itself awfully abstract. We have not mentioned Christ, who slams reality into place around us in a way that makes all talk about existence and being seem like evasions. I call myself a Christian because those abstract ideas about God are not enough. They don't touch suffering, about which we have much to discuss, and they don't take into account human relationships—like this one, for instance, this groping for God via email between two friends, in which the shared act of our longing, however different we seem from each other, is everything. You might say I am a Christian *despite* my understanding of God. Because I have known Christ.

"If I could love and trust the bare goodness of God, I would be free no matter what happened in my life." What a beautiful sentence and thought. I feel its truth so deeply, even though I don't quite know its origin. Certainly not the Bible. You say that "God has no interest of God's own that God pursues in any way at the expense of any creature." This can't be true of the God of the Bible, can it? God advocates rape, infanticide, and either initiates or participates in other forms of cruelty that would certainly seem to come at a high cost to other creatures. (The whole book of Job, for instance.) I'm not one to think of the Bible as the most reliable guide to God—it is one way among many—but I feel I'm misunderstanding something here.

You mention the transplant. This goes to the very heart of that Heschel quote above. I've written these paragraphs, as well as the previous letter, from a room in Mass General where my body has been subjected to various extremities in order to keep it a body, to keep me in it. People sometimes say that God becomes clearer in moments of suffering, but this is not necessarily true. What becomes clear is one's *longing* for God. Everything is stripped away, and very little else seems to matter. After living with cancer for twenty years, I have been too close to death too many times to fear that anymore. What I fear is dying without God. These letters help me feel God's presence, or at least the possibility of that.

Chris

MARCH 24

Dear Chris,

Last night my bad back woke me up, and, between 1:30 and 3:00, I was in a state between sleep and alertness. You were coming in and out of my hazy awareness—your understanding and experience of God, especially your fear of dying without God. My hypnagogic thoughts, summarized and ordered, went something like this: "Chris lives with an impossible God, a God he must bring into being and keep in being by acts of absolutely unmixed attention. That's why the crisis of his relation to his work, which is a consequence of severe illness, translates directly into the crisis of his relation to God. His body is assaulted and doing its utmost to fight a deadly intruder. He tries but he can neither bring God into being nor satisfy God's thirst. Brave man that he is, he doesn't fear death. He fears dying without God. His God is to blame for plaguing him with that fear, a god who loves himself first and who vanishes the moment Chris isn't able to express his love for him through whole-souled attention. He needs energies of life to sustain him, arms to hold him. And what does his God do? Does he take into his hands the clay that Chris, like all progeny of Adam, is, to breathe into him a breath of hope? No, his

God is threatening to leave him." Do you recognize yourself in any of this? Or is this merely a distorting charcoal sketch, drawn by the unfiltered stream of my nightly semiconsciousness?

In the morning, after making breakfast and chatting with Mira before she went to school, I was back to thinking about dying without God. This is impossible with the God of Jesus Christ, or so I believe, for nothing can separate us from the love of Christ and from God, as Paul writes in Romans. God abandons no one in the hour of their death. Like you, I love Moltmann's book *The Crucified God*, but I reject its central claim that God the Father abandoned Jesus on the cross. Hanging on the cross, Jesus was doing God's will, as he says in Gethsemane. For God to abandon him would have been monstrous. Instead, Jesus *felt* abandoned, and expressed this feeling in the cry of dereliction: "My God, my God, why have you forsaken me?" Lack of felt presence isn't absence. Throughout the ordeal, God was with Jesus, and at the end of it, God was there to receive back the breath of his life. God will be the liveliness even of our very last breath—as God will be the liveliness of our eyes opening to behold the resurrection beauty. Our pain, our incapacities, our disappointments, our anger, our dying itself may make us feel like motherless children (to echo the Black spiritual that starts with the same phrase), but we are never actually Godless, I believe. Nothing we do or fail to do can make God absent. Sure, I want more for the hour of my death than a nonabsent God. When the final night, all its stars extinguished, starts falling, I, too, want also to *feel* God's presence.

Can one find bare goodness in the Bible? I think it is in the book of Job, though the claim may seem absurd, given that God let the Adversary take away everything from Job and afflict him with unbearable pain. When we taught the class on suffering, you made the point that it makes for better poetry to lop off the first two and the last chapters of the book, the narrative introduction and conclusion that frame the poetry: Job's protest, his friends' moralizing defense of God, God's response from the whirlwind. I agree with your literary judgment. But the religious—theological and, above all, human—loss of disregarding the narrative framing is significant. In the first chapter, the Adversary issues what must be among the most significant challenges to faith in God's goodness. Does Job, righteous, wealthy, and widely honored, serve God "for nothing," or is his service self-interested, rendered to receive the blessing and protection God has given him? The book is sometimes described as theodicy, justification of God, but it is in fact justification of

Job, an anthropodicy. The whole ordeal is designed to show that Job, honest and at times near-irreverent as he was, loves God not for the goods he receives from God but for no other reason than that God is the highest good. Whether rich or poor, healthy or sick, it is a precarious life that one lives with this commitment. Its paradoxical promise is that it "pays" to love God for nothing; those who love God for nothing don't end up with nothing. Kierkegaard made a similar point about Abraham in *Fear and Trembling*. As I see it, Abraham and Job are two Hebrew Bible figures who loved "the bare, unfelt goodness that is hidden in God." So did Jesus, as the double "*my* God, *my* God" of the cry of dereliction suggests.

God often seems to us highly intrusive, issuing commands without considering our wishes. But, strange as it may seem, unlike many of God's representatives on Earth, God has no interests of God's own, only the interests of creatures—their actual interests, which are not always their *perceived* interests. I take the idea about God not having interests of God's own from Rowan Williams, though I cannot recall where in his writings I encountered it and I am not certain that I am using it in exactly his sense. From the idea that *God is love*—not appetitive love, craving the good that would please God, but unconditional, gift-bestowing love, bringing forth each creature and bestowing good upon it—it follows that God cannot be against any creature but is always only for it. From the idea that *God has no needs*, it follows that God doesn't have special interests that God would need to pursue at the expense of the good of any creature. I know, you can get the very opposite impression when reading central portions of the Bible. God often seems to be guarding God's own glory with fierce jealousy and deadly force. But then there is Christ, who discloses that God's glory is God's self-giving love.

At the end of this long letter, I should note that I completely agree with Heschel that we should not separate claims about God from the realities of lived faith (except that I don't understand its very end, the comment about the divine in the soul being "within reach of all thoughts"). I am here trying to articulate what's contained in my living faith and, at times, some conditions of its possibility. The conviction that God is not dependent on me, that, though I can think of God only in worldly categories, God exists (whatever "exists" means here) apart from the world—that conviction is internal to the very act of my faith and not an abstraction. How could I ultimately trust what needs a certain quality of my attention to come into being? How could I love such a god above all things, above my life itself? How could I know that such a god loves me along with all other creatures? How could I get comfort from such a god in the hour of my death? How could such a god be God?

Miroslav

PS. "Because I have known Christ," you write. I hope we return to this sentence at some point soon. I want to know what made you want to know Christ. What is it that you came to know about yourself and about God when you came to know Christ? What do you do with *his* God who was so central to his identity—the God of his people, the God of the Hebrew Bible, who, as you noted in your last letter, on its pages too often seems so unseemly?

MARCH 29

Dear Miroslav,

My grandmother died when she was eighty and I was twenty-two. We were very close, and I was with her when she died. It was one of the worst experiences of my life. When I think of a "whole-souled faith," it's her I'm thinking of, though she never "thought" about faith, per se, never read a book about it, certainly wouldn't understand any of the arguments we are now having.

She died utterly without God. With a kind of bare fear and elemental loneliness that seemed obscene. Are we really warranted in standing outside of that experience and saying that in fact it was her *perception* that was the problem? I can't do that, nor do I think anyone should. She was expressing the kind of absolute absence and spiritual destitution that is at the heart of religious thought for the past century—that is at the heart of Christianity, I would say, as any god worth our attention must include this level of bereft. The fact is, *many, many* people die without God. "How could I get comfort from such a god in the hour of my death?" you ask. You might not. It might prove very helpful to have a conception of God that included that reality, a faith that would not be pulverized by circumstance. "How could such a god be God?" This is the question I am trying to live into.

I think you make too much of these moments of inspiration and attention—no doubt because I have not been clear enough. What Weil says is that any "absolutely unmixed attention is *prayer*." (Italics mine.) Of course, there are many other ways to God—as many ways, in fact, as there are people. God is not static, and faith is always finding new forms. "How could I ultimately trust what needs a certain quality of my attention to come into being?" you ask. How could you trust anything else? There is not some static entity "out there" like a rock you look away from. (The physicist Carlo Rovelli argues there is not even that rock; matter itself exists only in relation.) Even the way you formulate the dynamic, loving a god "above all things, above [your] life itself" is an act of imagination.

I remember once in that class on suffering that we taught I asked you if you'd ever truly felt the absence of God. You paused for a long time and then said, "No." I can't tell you how shocked I was, as my own experience of God has been so fraught with (and fueled by!) God's absence. Would you still answer the question in the same way? I ask only because of what you wrote (so beautifully) several letters ago:

> In the space where God was present to me, there is—nothing. My life continues in its inertias, but at the edge of my experiences, I sense a cosmic motherlessness.

I think the suffering of Jesus is at the very heart of Christianity and is the source of its power. I think Jesus suffered exactly what my grandmother suffered, the absolute absence of God. If not, he's not fully human, and his life remains a model and example rather than a visceral kin we can cling to in our hearts.

All that said, I am aware of a certain masochistic element in my definition of faith, or at least the possibility of that. Your last letter has been an agony for me because I have been unable to type an answer. For several days I had to wear a monitor on one hand to make sure that the doses of pain medicines didn't kill me. (I sometimes hear other patients' alarms going off in rooms nearby.) I was eager to answer because I felt a certain combativeness and/or supercilious pity ("Poor Chris and his false God, etc.") in your letter. Balked, anxious, and needing someone to talk to, I sent our whole exchange to Danielle, who said that your letters all seemed full of love and candid care, whereas *my own* seemed a bit combative and defensive at times. And then she wrote me this:

> When you are married to someone who is chronically—and at times, you believe, fatally—ill you are always up against the denial that their suffering, and your own suffering, *mean*.
>
> In the worst case this is the result of callousness: the impulse to look away from that which one finds depressing, ugly, or boring. More often it's a coping mechanism; denying another's suffering and all of its painful specificity (particularly that of a family member) protects you from your own fragility.
>
> Often it's a very well-intentioned impulse, even a loving one, that denies the extent and intensity of a loved one's suffering. It comes from the fact that you don't want them (or yourself) to suffer.
>
> Also: We're helpless. We deny it because we can't do anything about it.
>
> But if we don't deny it and still acknowledge that we

can't fix it, if we realize that we are not in control of our loved ones' suffering but are still desperate to end it, we might be inclined to pray. It's at that point that we are most at risk of being put in a false position with regard to language.

The risk of falsity isn't because God isn't real—the urge and the willingness to pray have already announced themselves. The risk is in the fact that the movement of faith, of the heart towards surrender, happens at the point that we can no longer tolerate, or make meaning of, or find words for, reality.

In one way, to pray at such a moment is simply humility, an expression of faith. However, for a poet, whatever rote or spontaneous-but-approximate prayer one utters at such a moment is also aware of its failure as language. For a poet, prayers, psalms, beatitudes, every form of assurance that seeks to blunt or smooth or banish an edge of agony without first acknowledging it and witnessing its immediate particulars is, on some level, an act of doubt rather than faith. If we believe we can be touched by grace, we must believe that touch can travel through all the interstices of pain we've earned simply by having had them forced on us. Grace can only obliterate pain that has been revealed, shown, known.

This is the needle a true poem threads: It acknowledges the extremity of a person's pain, while believing in the word, the sound, the phrase that can name and answer—and thus alleviate—it.

Every writer knows this feeling: A physical or existential anguish being answered and thus ended (albeit temporarily) by the arrival of a word; of *the* word that is sometimes so uncannily satisfying, so right, so affirming of one's entire life, so anticatastrophic, such a reversal of the entire mechanism of misery that has driven one's mind and body and soul to that point, that one cannot help but call it divine. That's the word that completes the poem and renews one's life as a poet. For when completeness comes what is in part will disappear.

Such a poem may be one of the purest forms of prayer. Yet, just because we are poets who understand the value of the absolute right word (no matter how esoteric it might be), we can't become literary fundamentalists who assume that because a word has been corrupted

> by misuse, or overuse, that the concept is null and void. The ubiquity and banality of a word like "blessed" (or: #blessed) and the whole devalued faith it represents does nothing to alleviate our need to receive God's blessing. We can't fall into the trap of thinking that our own blessing will be so new and idiosyncratic that it would be unrecognizable to the Old Testament fathers.
>
> Though it might be different in substance, in texture, in particulars—though the right words for it might be different—we have to be humble enough to assume that the spiritual experience of "being blessed" by God will be the same. Like Falstaff's sought-after gift of "More Life" the essence here is the utter supplication and the over-the-top giftedness: the movement (the verb), not the content (the nouns and the adjectives). We might need to invent new words to describe these things, but we also need to accept that our spiritual situation is not that different from that of the past—nor is our God a different God.

You see why I remain so helplessly in love after all these years. (The subject line of this email is: "Spiritual genius droppin' on your dome pate.")

Danielle's email gets to the heart of what I have been trying to say. That the path to God is always new; that every generation, indeed every person, must "recreate" its god, or at least its notion of what God is. But she also preserves and insists on the connection between the present and the past. One of my favorite moments from Anna Kamieńska's diaries is when she says, "I want only with my whole self to reach the heart of obvious truths." I am sometimes in danger of forgetting the obvious truths. One of which is that the God I worship is the same God worshipped by Bonhoeffer, Luther, Augustine, Paul. (Though how barren the tradition seems in terms of women, whose modern and contemporary contributions have so greatly influenced my own thinking.)

Or the writer of the book of Job, for that matter. You say that you agree with me that Job is superior aesthetically without its last chapter but that nonetheless you prefer the theological message of the whole. As my earlier letters make clear, that seems to me an impossible position to hold. The book of Job is in poetry for several reasons. It precludes resolution, for one thing. It enacts, rather than explains, the shock of God. Certainly it is no theodicy, as you say. It reads to me as both a scream and a prayer, both things at once. "Nothing but grief could permit newness," Walter Brueggemann writes of the prophets. "Only a poem could bring the grief to notice." The same could be said of Job.

The postscript to Job is, of course, in prose. It feels like the work of a man who couldn't bear the truth of what he had just read. It is the equivalent to the versions of Lear that dominated eighteenth- and nineteenth-century productions, in which Lear and Cordelia are reunited at the end and happiness wins. Or the end of Mark, for that matter, which is an obvious flinch from the austere conclusion of the genuine Gospel. Job is great precisely because it speaks the truth about God, which includes darkness and suffering and what seems like pure absurdity. (All those members of Job's first family, for instance, were they simply collateral casualties for Job's illumination?) And what is that truth? A scream and a prayer.

This letter is far too long, but I don't want to end with that note of darkness and destitution. Absence is one way we seem called to experience God, especially in the times we are now in. But there is abundance, too. There is receiving a letter from my wife that reminds me of all that I love in her. There is writing a letter to my friend who loves me enough to think about me during his sleepless nights. There is my daughter coming into this grim hospital room and filling the nurses' noticeboard with jokes to make me laugh. There is grace in my life, if I can just keep my eyes open enough to see it.

On Having Mis-Identified a Wildflower

A thrush, because I'd been wrong,
Burst rightly into song
In a world not vague, not lonely,
Not governed by me only.

—Richard Wilbur

Chris

APRIL 3

Dear Chris,

Before sending off my last letter, I was debating with myself for a while whether to include my midnight doubts about your God or not. I was afraid that you might sense in them what you originally did: supercilious pity. As Danielle wrote, my candor, perhaps misguided, was meant as an expression of care. But it's not always easy to keep condescension and care apart; it isn't much easier to keep them apart for the giver than for the recipient. We are friends, and if unawares any condescension slithered into my care, I hope you would forgive me. It was not meant to be there. On my part, I sensed no combativeness in your letters, but intensity appropriate to the importance of the subject and whose absence would make our correspondence less meaningful to me.

I risked including my rather pointed questioning because in what you wrote about bringing God into being I sensed, perhaps wrongly, something of a Rilke-like aspiration: the absolute poet seeking to help a helpless God, to keep God alive. Addressing God, in the *Book of Hours*, Rilke writes:

You, neighbor God, if sometimes in the long night
I rouse you with my loud pounding,—
it's only that I so seldom hear you breathing
and know: you're in that huge room alone.
And should you need something, no one is there
to lift water to your lips.
I listen always. Give a small sign.
Feel me here.

—Translated by
Edward Snow

Rilke's poor God is dependent on the poet's pity—arrogant and supercilious pity?—and not merely for help. Without the poet, God just isn't. "What will you do, God, when I die?" Rilke asks in the same text, and continues:

I am your jug (and I will shatter)
I am your drink (and I'll go bad)
I am your clothing and your calling,
you'll lose all reason, losing me

With me gone, you'll have no house
where warm words will welcome you.
Without me, you'll have no sandals:
your exhausted feet will wander bare.

Your mighty cloak will fall away.
Your gaze, which my cheek took in
soft and warm, like a pillow,
will arrive here, look, search long—
and finally at the end of sunset
lie down in the lap of alien stones.

What will you do, God? I'm afraid.

—Translated by
Edward Snow

That kind of fear for God—or was it Rilke's fear for himself?—seemed implicit in what you wrote about God. That's what I was resisting—and a kind of privatization of God. What do you make of these beautiful and powerful lines from Rilke? If I understand him rightly, he assumes the death of God. The poet, who brings God into being, has now replaced the prophet, who announces God's coming. That's *not* exactly what you are saying, though you do write about "recreating" God, even if in quotation marks. Do you think that the differing conceptions of God in Exodus, Isaiah, John, and Paul are distinct re-creations of God? That each of us makes our own? In one sense each of us does have our own God—as each of us lives in our own world. Imagination is involved in every act of perception. Our notions of God, too, are acts of imagination. But imagination, in this sense, does not make things out of nothing; it always works on what is before it, what is out there, what has existence independent from us. Imagination helps constitute what is apart from us as a phenomenon *for us*. I take it that Isaiah and St. John have distinct takes on one and the same God, or that these are differing self-revelations of the one God. By definition, the one God is the God of all—and also uniquely the God of each.

Etty Hillesum, whom we read together in the seminar on suffering, but about whose God we didn't talk much, returns in her diary repeatedly to Rilke, her favorite poet, and to the *Book of Hours* with its feeble God. "But one thing is becoming increasingly clear to me," she writes, addressing God, "that You cannot help us, that we must help You to help ourselves."

In critical months of the Amsterdam Nazi occupation and her difficult Westerbork internment, the company of such a helpless God gave her almost superhuman strength. At the very end, in a cattle car headed to Auschwitz, she was able to sing and help her family sing, even though she was clear-eyed about what was waiting for them. To me, she was a true saint (though some think of her as a foolish masochist, and I don't have ironclad arguments that she wasn't). So perhaps I was wrong in suggesting that a God who needs our help and who abandons us cannot be of much help in the hour of our death. Though, when I read her diaries, I see her oscillating between the God of the Bible, before whom she kneels and on whom she radically relies, and Rilke's infirm God, whom she must help nearly as much as she must help her hunted and murdered people. She seems to be embracing both of these seemingly irreconcilable visions of God. Like Danielle and you. I respect that. To me, though, such neediness and helplessness compromise God's divinity; they impede more than set free God's love, which is God's very being. But that's because I think that the God of Abraham and of Jesus, not a helpless deity, is not nearly as dead as is often thought.

Which brings me to the language of faith, to faith's "sayability," and to God's coming to be, or, as I would prefer, to be *for us*. We repeatedly touched on the question of language, and Danielle helpfully moved our discussion forward. I am of divided mind. I can unequivocally affirm the great value of "the right word," for which the kind of skill and attention you described earlier are indispensable. All of my life I have been nourished by "right words." But I grew up in a Pentecostal church where, as you know well, folks spoke in heavenly tongues that neither they nor anybody else understood. In my early teens, I despised the practice—in prayer meeting after prayer meeting, simpleminded old women and men repeating what turned out to be the same short speech in tongues. I would mock them by reciting word for word their incomprehensible speeches. In the meantime, though, I have come to believe that, even at our best, when we speak about God, we always speak in tongues, not quite understanding what we are saying. Our prayers and all our speech about God *always* "fails as language," as Danielle put it, and when it succeeds, it does so notwithstanding this failure. God must come into religious language for it to actually speak, for it to become about God and to become God's speech.

When it comes to religious language, I wonder whether we shouldn't attend more to lives well lived than to words just rightly spoken. Do not saintly lives help words that fail as language succeed as communication? I saw it happen with my nanny: The joy of her life, brimming with patient love, rescued flat words and kitschy songs from triteness, filled them with arresting meaning. That's how I experience Jesus, too, though in his case, the "inadequacy" of speech isn't kitschiness but ordinariness. What I need is openness or, even better, a kind of watchfulness, so that, when the Bridegroom comes, I am not found sleeping.

There is another way in which the right words may matter less than we tend to think. "Grace can only obliterate pain that has been revealed, shown, known," writes Danielle compellingly. That's how grace works for many of us, especially in late modernity with our sense of how trauma, memory, and healing are related. I don't want to take anything away from her claim, except "only." In the paradigmatic case of grace at work in the Bible, in Exodus, the pain is "known, shown, revealed," not because those who experience it have articulated it or because someone else has articulated it for them, but because God heard their inarticulate groans and cries, remembered the covenant, and came to their rescue. In Romans 8, one of the most important texts in the New Testament, Paul echoes Exodus's way of relating affliction, its articulation—or lack of it—and salvation. He zeroes in on "groaning" and uses the same Greek word as does the Septuagint in Exodus. After noting the groaning of the nonhuman creation, he continues: "We ourselves . . . groan inwardly while we wait for . . . the redemption of our bodies . . . Likewise, the Spirit helps us in our weakness; for we do not know how to pray as we ought, but that very Spirit intercedes with sighs too deep for words." The Spirit can inhabit inarticulacy. As you can imagine, I find this immensely comforting.

Poets and theologians, each in their own way, are in the word business. It's a great business; I have certainly loved it my whole life and every day of it. God uses our words—sometimes. But God doesn't depend on them. Neither does our salvation. Some of the most important things in life happen wordlessly.

I have to end this letter, and I have not written about two important comments in your last letter, about my experience of God's absence and about Job's "scream and prayer." I have some thoughts.

Miroslav

APRIL 11

Dear Miroslav,

Easter Sunday! I should be leaving Boston this week and should know if this treatment has worked. I just livestreamed a sermon by a friend who quoted Austin Farrer: "We do not come to God for a little help, a little support to our own good intentions. We come to God for resurrection." Amen.

The truth is I believe in a God that died just as we die—alone, bereft, once and for all—and I believe in a God that broke free from that static tragedy and thereby transformed forever what we understand death to be and what we understand life to be. I believe we do in fact each create the God we serve, and I believe that underlying all of those creations is a singular being that is available and indivisible and constant for all of us. I believe that you and I have come to Christianity simply because it was the religion in which we were raised, and I believe that we are Christians because it is our fate. (How I love Paul Ricoeur's definition of faith: chance raised to the level of a destiny by virtue of a constant choice.) I believe there is no one truth, and yet we must wager everything on the one that claims us.

Obviously, as my entries above make all too clear, I am not *comfortable* living in these paradoxes, but I am becoming—how should I say—native to them. A stranger to the earth, as Marianne Moore says, but reconciled.

Thanks for bringing in the Rilke poem. It's powerful because it precisely reverses the standard relation between believer and God. Instead of us wondering how we will live without God, the poem asks how God will live without us. Instead of our agony over God's nonexistence, the poet worries about his own and what that will mean for God.

It is a *poem*, though, not a work of theology. It renders experience rather than describing it. For me, the experience is quite familiar. I do often feel as if we (all of us, throughout all history and encompassing all religions) are sustaining a kind of empty fiction. Sometimes I feel this is the case simply because there is no God, and we are all self-deluded dupes. More often I feel it's because all of the ways we have learned to approach and define God are not simply inadequate but positively misguided. That we need to start over.

But then sometimes I am shattered by the reality of God. Sometimes I really do experience Farrer's sense of resurrection.

As did Rilke, I think. It's important to remember that the same poet who wrote the lines you quote also wrote, in the very same book, these:

> Only for the child does it dawn.
> Only as a child am I sure,
> after so much fear, so much night,
> you are not gone.
> Every time I try to measure
> how deep, how long, how far—
> you are and are and are,
> time trembling around you.
>
> It is as if at once I were
> infant, boy, man, more.
> To feel: only the circle is rich
> with return.
>
> Thank you, deep power,
> which always more softly,
> and behind so many walls,

creates with me.
The day's labor grows plain
as a face, holy,
to my dark hands.

—Translated by the authors

This poem merges the God of transcendence and the God of immanence, the God that is beyond all of our efforts to conjure and connect with him and the God that is in "the day's labor." Is it a definitive statement about God? No, it is a poem, like the book of Job, teasingly intelligible, immune to summary and paraphrase, reality and mystery merged.

The essence of those lines from Rilke you quote is that God is vulnerable. You asked some time ago what experience of Christ I had that made me think of myself as a Christian. This is one. Once when I was suffering terribly and near death Christ came to me and was not simply near me but *was* me, in my prayers and in the interactions I had with friends and family and in the very air I breathed. Living and hoping and—this most of all—suffering. I take this to be a fundamental lesson that Christ reveals of God's nature. God experienced and experiences suffering just as we do, from loneliness to grief, from physical pain to death. That traditional notion of God as self-sufficient, some adamantine entity who is concerned for but ultimately impervious to us—I reject this. I'm with Teresa: God's on this journey with us.

I like what you say about valuing lives over words. I am never not pierced and restored by thinking of Bonhoeffer's statement that Christ is always stronger in our brother's heart than in our own. And Rowan Williams has a sermon in which he says that there are lives that speak to us as no precept ever can. They reveal to us a peace and promise we want for ourselves. And the specific life he's talking about in that sermon? Etty Hillesum. The paradox in that instance, though, is that we wouldn't *have* that life without the words. "There must be someone to live through it all," she says, "and bear witness to the fact that God lived, even in these times." God *needed* her, not to keep himself alive, not in the Rilkean sense, but to keep alive the means of perceiving God among a destroyed people. And there is an even sharper turn of the knife: We wouldn't care about the life were her words not so beautifully formed, her perceptions so fresh. Her aesthetic triumph enables the moral one. Technique is the test of sincerity.

And speaking of exemplary lives and exemplary art, yesterday

I had coffee with Fanny Howe, whose work has meant more to me than any other living writer. I told her about this exchange, and we talked some about our conceptions of God. At one point she said, "But I don't know. I don't know anything at all. I just try to live toward God." An eighty-year-old woman sitting in a small dark apartment with makeshift bookshelves and a bed in the living room, this singular and still-burning mind with a lifetime of contemplation and devotion behind her. I don't know. I don't know anything at all.

I never feel as if I'm at some crossroads trying to decide whether or not to follow God. That decision has long ago been made. I could no more turn away from God than I could decide to stop breathing. What I do wish, though, is that I could get out of my own way more often, that gift and grace could be more purely aligned. Here is a nineteenth-century poem I find myself saying to myself quite often:

> Not the round natural world, not the deep mind,
> The reconcilement holds: the blue abyss
> Collects it not; our arrows sink amiss
> And but in Him may we our import find.
> The agony to know, the grief, the bliss

Of toil, is vain and vain: clots of the sod
Gathered in heat and haste and flung behind
To blind ourselves and others, what but this
Still grasping dust and sowing toward the wind?
No more thy meaning seek, thine anguish plead,
But leaving straining thought and stammering word,
Across the barren azure pass to God;
Shooting the void in silence like a bird,
A bird that shuts his wings for better speed.

—Frederick Goddard
Tuckerman, "Sonnet
XXVIII"

Chris

PS. I want to hear about your feelings of/for God's absence, but let me end with a moment of deep and utter presence. Of resurrection, even. It is now two days after Easter. Yesterday Danielle and I sat with the doctors in a conference room in a Boston hospital, the kind of room in which you often get dire news, and learned that this treatment I have undergone, this experimental procedure that I am one of the first people in the world with my disease to receive, has worked. After so assiduously preparing to die, it seems I must learn to live again. We drove home surrounded by God, filled with God, the barren azure grown almost unbearably bright around us. And I thought of Rilke:

> Into them [God's hands] I place these fragments, my life,
> and you, God—spend them however you want.

APRIL 18

Dear Chris,

Yes, reflection on God's absence can wait. It's time to celebrate God's actual presence. Liturgically, the Easter season lasts seven weeks; forty-nine days to celebrate Christ's presence (after which comes Ordinary Time, also a time of presence: the Spirit's). It is such a beautiful thing that your own resurrection—your own realization that you had been taken out of a likely grave—happened so close to Easter. The news of it caused a great rejoicing in the Dwelle/Volf household. Like you and Danielle, we, too, felt that God answered our prayers, and, with life-giving power, came to be so near to us, too. Imagine me writing this letter with champagne in hand.

To describe the conquest of a deadly illness as "resurrection" is to use a metaphor, of course, which is *not* to say that Farrer was wrong that we come to God, ultimately, hoping for resurrection. The New Testament makes a distinction between raising the dead and resurrection. The difference is not simply that the first is a return to ordinary life whereas the second is a transposition into another, everlasting, form of life. Importantly, though an event in the life of an individual, resurrection is an eschatological reality that is inextricably tied to the new life of the whole world. Was Jesus not raised as an individual? one could object. In *The Crucified God*, Moltmann makes an important distinction between resurrection *from* the dead and resurrection *of* the dead. Jesus was raised from the dead, but he was raised, Moltmann argues, as the first of all those who had died. Resurrection as a universal, planetary event: Each of us is raised as ourselves and all are raised together into a new world.

What struck me when I was reading the first paragraph of your letter is that, in a localized, circumscribed way, an enmeshment of the one and many happened also on the second day after Easter this year, when you were raised to new life. Danielle and the girls, Jessica and I, along with your many other friends, were raised, too. An individual event was a communal event. Who God was for you became who God was for all of us because our lives are mutually implicated. If we make a giant metaphysical leap—an eschatological one, too—we land in the vicinity of the idea that my God can be truly *God* only as the God of all; inversely, only the God of all can properly be my God.

This is how I understand your claim that the one God who is uniquely each person's own is simultaneously "constant for us all." If so, there are significant constraints for how we each "create"—I must put the quotation marks—the God we serve. There are so many ways to go wrong, occasionally very wrong, with our own personal and collective theogonies. I go wrong many times in my own "making" of my God. That might be my great sin in relation to God: crafting God to serve the need, my need, of the hour. What is your take on such religious (and nonreligious!) mis-makings? What makes the God I make truly divine—and the God of all?

I suspect that you know where I am going with this. Straight to Martin Luther. He was uncompromising about God's oneness (and therefore God's universality) and yet he believed that each of us makes our own God. He didn't keep that conviction tucked away in some scholarly disputation to be read by the enlightened but put it right at the very beginning of his *Large Catechism*, a basic instruction manual for all ministers. "What does it mean to have a god?" Or, "What is God?" he asks. The answer:

> A "god" is the term for that to which we are to look for all good and in which we are to find refuge in all need. Therefore, to have a god is nothing else than to trust and believe in that one with your whole heart. As I have often said, it is the trust and faith of the heart alone that make both God and an idol.

Ludwig Feuerbach could easily find in Luther a precursor of his thesis that God is a desirable human stretched out into infinity and dwelling in eternity. Feuerbach did not distinguish between God and idols; God was an idol, a mere human product. Luther thought that the entire edifice of Christian faith depended more on that distinction—between God and idol—than on the distinction between faith and its absence. Following the passage quoted above, Luther continues:

> If your faith and trust are right, then God is the true one. Conversely, where your trust is false and wrong, there you do not have the true God. For these two belong together, faith and God. Anything on which your heart relies and depends, I say, that is really your God.

How does one distinguish between the two, God and an idol? For Luther, this is the most important question a human can ask. Whom or what should we trust and love above all things or, in the terminology of Paul Tillich, who or what is the worthy object of our ultimate concern? The true God is revealed on the cross, Luther believed. God looks "weak" and "foolish" and "disfigured," as Jesus did hanging on the cross outside the city gate. This is a window to a God who didn't aspire to be glorious, but out of an unusual kind of love came down to rescue those who are weak, poor, bereft of beauty, unlovable . . . The One who loves that way is the true God, worthy of our trust and love. I think you and I agree on this.

You and I will likely continue to differ on the death of God. The contrast between the God who suffers and dies "just as we do" and the God who is "some adamantine entity . . . impervious to us" (what a beautiful and precise description!) seems to me too crude. That's how Moltmann, in more prosaic language, distinguishes his own position from classical theism, whose representatives, in turn, put the difference in the same way as well. I am not persuaded by either position. I see neither of the alternatives in the Hebrew Bible or in the New Testament. I am with Abraham Heschel and his idea of God's *pathos* as he develops it in *The Prophets*: God is affected by our suffering, but God doesn't suffer as we do. Instead, God experiences emotions—grief and anger and empathy, for instance—in a manner appropriate to the nature of God. And God certainly doesn't die. (Shai Held has a very good discussion of Heschel's divine pathos in *Abraham Joshua Heschel: The Call of Transcendence*, his Harvard doctoral dissertation.) It may seem that the incarnation should make a difference in how Christians, as distinct from Jews, view God's suffering and death, but I don't think it does. Jesus suffered like us as a human; but he suffered *un*like us as God.

Now, I can see how one can find comfort in a God who suffers and dies just as we do, especially if one has suffered greatly: God shares in our destiny and ennobles it; God understands our pain from within. We are one with God in our suffering. But to me, as to Nietzsche, a dead God is a dead God, and then one has to sail on a raging sea without any hope of firm land. The only poem I know that explicitly invokes the crucified God is by nineteenth-century Serbian poet Aleksa Šantić. I wish I could translate it; I am quite fond of it. At its beginning and end, it describes with harsh musicality the falling of the night, the rugged tip of a black rock putting out the last reddish ray ("*Vrh hridi crne / Trne / Zadnji rumeni zrak*," each "r" a rolling one). In its middle, emaciated heads ("*mršave glave*") kneel before the aphasic crucified God, pleading in vain. If God is dead, who will raise God? I don't think it works to say that the first divine Person raises the second divine Person, for then you end up with two gods.

I have almost come to the point of writing about my experience of the peculiar kind of absence of God that I see when

Christ was crucified. But I am still celebrating the marvelous event that happened on the second day of this year's Easter. I wrote all this under the wise sign of Fanny Howe's confession you mention, "But I don't know. I don't know anything at all. I just try to live toward God." I just try to live and think toward God's coming to the world.

Yesterday evening I thought this letter was done, and then, in the middle of the night, I thought about Hillesum—how her extraordinary life and her splendid technique formed a unity. In her diary, crafting sentences and crafting herself were one and the same process of acting and writing herself into holiness. And, as you put so well, she was what God used—and in that sense, needed—"to keep alive the means of perceiving God among a destroyed people." I love her words, her craft. But I would not have read nearly as many of her words nor enjoyed any of them as much, had it not been for her life. Some ten years ago, when I was regularly reading short stories in *The New Yorker*, I read so many well-crafted texts that, for me, were worse than beautiful photographs of decaying cityscapes, which create voyeurs of its viewers, desensitizing them to the actual harm to which they bear witness. Many of these stories—and perhaps I exaggerate their number because I grew frustrated with them—were doing no more than making trivialities glitter. I've seen *evil* made to glitter, too, though not in *The New Yorker*. I cannot help but think that St. Paul didn't get it all wrong when he saw a tension, perhaps in some instances even incongruity, between the foolish and disfigured Christ and the wisdom and beauty of well-crafted words about that very foolishness and lack of beauty. Beauty and goodness are not inextricably bound, at least not in modernity; their unity depends on our holding them together.

The blend of life and literature in Hillesum's *Letters and Diaries*, the extremity of the time and seriousness of her life, made *her* beautiful to me; the beauty of her words is part of something much larger. This is how I experience your *My Bright Abyss* as well.

When I was a small child, I would run my fingers over my nanny's wrinkled face, tenderly, barely touching her skin, the way Mira sometimes touches my face or places a gentle kiss on my bald head. I am sixty-six years old, and when I remember my nanny today, I find myself sometimes wishing I could do it again—express with a gaze and a gentle touch the reverence I feel for her saintly life. Her conventionally un-beautiful face made beautiful by her life. I feel a bit like this toward Hillesum.

Her face, as seen, for example, in a particular photograph of her holding a cigarette (which in some reproductions does not appear because a misplaced piety had it erased from her hand), is for me something like an icon, though not in the modern sense, which has much more to do with fame than with holiness. Not in the classical Orthodox sense, either.

A week or so ago, I read Bruce Foltz's book *The Noetics of Nature*, the main point of which is that we should relate to nature as to an icon. In the process, he contrasts, as do many Orthodox writers, the schematic faces of Orthodox icons and the realistic faces of Renaissance religious art. Icons, he claims, are windows that let us see God; Renaissance faces draw our gaze to themselves, at best illustrating elements of a sacred story. As I see it, neither the window-face nor the illustration-face suffices. The concrete their-ness of the face to whom it belongs is precisely what matters. The her-ness of Hillesum's life, present to me through literature and centered on her face, is what moves me, a unity of literary beauty and arduously lived goodness.

Miroslav

APRIL 27

Dear Miroslav,

That's beautifully put—God at once singular and shared, utterly specific to one life and mind and yet encompassing, too, all life, all minds. That was my experience of this illness and healing. I have felt over the past few months quite close to God, the God that is *my God*, the one I have been trying to describe in these letters, the one who seems, sometimes, not to be your God. And yet I have also felt, during the illness but especially after the healing, a *shared* divinity, a grace and love and rescue that included you and many others.

Two of my oldest friends came to stay with me in Boston during this ordeal. One is a Jewish Buddhist, the other a secular seeker with a deep antipathy to organized religion but a strong feeling for myth and mystery. The whole experience brought me wonderfully, almost painfully close to each of them—"painfully" both because we are not used to, and hardly equipped for, the intense intimacy that imminent death can enable, and also simply because I knew that, one way or another, it would end. Life can't be sustained at that pitch—nor should we want it so.

But it's the healing and its aftermath that made all this clear to me, the joy that went through me and them, like an electric impulse, from heart to heart of all those who have been involved—which is what you describe so beautifully. It was God. Is God. I can easily see the whole emotional event in trinitarian terms. God is the mysterious but undeniable energy pulsing through the hearts and minds of all of us, the sense of a *general* rescue and a blessed release from all definitions; Christ is my two friends sitting by my bed for over a month, is all the other friends and family praying and grieving and finally rejoicing, is the brute and blessed fact of life and death; and the Spirit is the overpowering intuition that lets these realities breathe and be—and be *one*.

But I have no need to see any of this in specifically Christian terms. My two friends—indeed, most of my friends—are not Christian, as I say, but I am sure they would recognize the emotional and *spiritual* exchange that you and I have described.

I do take the metaphor—and, of course, it's a metaphor—of the trinity very seriously. It seems to me one of the two greatest imaginative insights of Christianity (the other being incarnation). But I can't reconcile my understanding of the trinity with your depiction of the crucifixion. Jesus either is God or he isn't. The cross is all or nothing. To say that Jesus is God but then to somehow separate God from Jesus at the moment of the crucifixion makes no sense to me. (The God Jesus prayed to is the God we pray to, sometimes intimate, inseparable from our very selves, sometimes remote, merely a word that taunts and haunts at the same time.) I realize it's philosophically preposterous to say that God died and somehow resurrected himself, though I don't find it any more preposterous than thinking of God having a "son." In any event, I would avoid that phrasing—"God resurrecting himself"—and even that understanding. Indeed there is no *understanding* to be had here, but there is truth, one which accords with human experience of God (atheists are *right* in this regard, though blind to every resurrection) and with the spark of darkness that abides within absolute despair.

Believe me, I feel the offense to reason, the razory implacable paradox. And feel the deep hydraulic draw of that. Lev Shestov suggested that "contradiction is one of the signs that make us recognize that we are approaching the final truth, for it shows that man no longer feels the fear which ordinary criteria inspire in him." I am trying very hard to articulate an idea while remaining true to it.

As for the danger of each person creating their own God, of course it's there, and I agree completely with Luther and Tillich that the primary question one faces in this life is that of idolatry or ultimate concern. (I do appreciate the way you've merged these two theologies into versions of one thing.) But just because we recognize the danger doesn't mean it can be avoided. I think even within the most fundamental sects each believer is in fact creating his or her own God. That's simply the nature of imagination and our relation to reality. Of course, the degree of difference may be much greater among other groups of believers—canvass most liberal Protestant church parishioners these days and I think you'll find very little consistency of belief, even regarding the major tenets of Christianity—but the dynamic is the same.

What do we do about it? Nothing. Muddle on as best we can, which is precisely what Christians have been doing for centuries, though I have always found this little poem by Richard Wilbur a helpful guide in this regard:

Teresa

After the sun's eclipse,
The brighter angel and the spear which drew
A bridal outcry from her open lips,
She could not prove it true,
Nor think at first of any means to test
By what she had been wedded or possessed.

Not all cries were the same;
there was an island in mythology
Called by the very vowels of her name
Where vagrants of the sea,
Changed by a wand, were made to squeal and cry
As heavy captives in a witch's sty.

The proof came soon and plain:
Visions were true which quickened her to run
God's barefoot errands in the rocks of Spain
Beneath its beating sun,
And lock the O of ecstasy within
The tempered consonants of discipline.

This poem says two things. First: The test of vision is action. Revelations are proved within relations. (Luther's whole life is a testament to this.) Any mystical experience of God—and Simone Weil thought that mystical experience of God was the *only* possible experience of God—is valid only insofar as it leads to Christ (though I think Christ is available to, and at work in, people who do not believe in him). And second: There is a constant, difficult, productive tension between imagination (the ecstasy) and tradition (the discipline). Any tilt too far in one direction unbalances belief.

I feel uneasy arguing theology with you—not simply because I know less than you do (though there is that) but because I feel a rift between my explanations and my experience. I wouldn't even be a religious person were it not for poetry, which has not only repeatedly brought me into contact with an *other*, but has seemed to demand something of me in its wake—very like Teresa's visions. But poetry remains perpetually open. God moves through art but doesn't get stuck there. I sometimes think he gets stuck in theology—fixed, frozen, and therefore inevitably falsified.

I have been thinking a lot of Rilke since you brought him up. He was a crucial figure for Hillesum, probably *the* crucial figure along with the doctor/wrestling partner (!) who was so instrumental in helping her find herself and her voice. In one way, this makes perfect sense given the God that Rilke addresses and erases in his poetry, the God that has no name, is outside of religion and reachable only through mystical experiences. In another sense, though, Rilke is an odd choice for Hillesum, since Rilke separated art and life so absolutely and lived as if the former were of paramount importance. American literary culture has turned Rilke into a flowery "spiritual" writer, but there is something hard and arctic about Rilke's work ("an emotionally untainted sense of form" is how the art critic Edgar Wind described it). I love it and have learned a great deal from it about both art and life. I do find Rilke quite cold, though, basically the opposite of Hillesum, who not only is everywhere *warm* in her writings but who also, as you say, so thoroughly fused art and life.

As for that distinction between relating to nature as an icon or an illustration, Rilke would say that the whole problem lies in the word "relate." We don't relate to nature. We *are* nature. That we see ourselves as separate, that we think of consciousness as a grasping action, a taking hold, an *understanding*—this is precisely what keeps us so frantic and sad.

> With all its eyes the animal world
> beholds the Open. Only ours
> are as if inverted and set all around it
> like traps at the doors to freedom.
> What's outside we know only from the animal's
> countenance: for almost from the first we take a child

and turn him around and force him to gaze
backward and take in structure, not the Open
that lies so deep in an animal's face. Free from death.
Only we see death; the free animal has its demise
perpetually behind it and always before it
God, and when it moves, it moves into eternity,
the way brooks and running springs move.
We, though: never, not for one day, do we
have that pure space ahead of us into which flowers
endlessly open. What we have is World
and always World and never Nowhere without the no:
that unguarded element one breathes
and *knows* endlessly and never craves. As a child
one gets lost there in the quiet, only to be
jostled back. Or someone dying *is* it.
For, close to death, one looks at death no longer
but instead stares *out*, perhaps with the wide gaze of animals.

—Translated by Edward Snow
(though I have "improved"
one important line!)

The poems we were referencing earlier were from Rilke's first book. This passage from *The Duino Elegies* is a truer representation of Rilke and his idea of the divine. God is what reality is constantly opening into. To have faith, to live *in* faith, is to share that existence, that constant opening. Christ falls away for Rilke, but I would say that Rilke's vision is only made possible by the incarnation. I would say the same thing about Etty Hillesum's translation of art to action, word to Word. I don't mean that she was an "anonymous Christian," to use Rahner's unfortunate term. I simply mean that I see the existence and power of Christ in her work in the camps. It needn't be named or claimed, that power; perhaps it is even more powerful, more fully itself, when it isn't.

I am deeply moved and aided by Rilke's vision of God. But I am also dissatisfied. Something in me demands—how to put it?—a bit more blood. Something in me, beyond the craveless state Rilke defines above, craves the reality (the divinity) that remains messy, and overflows art and contemplation, and includes great suffering and jags of transformative joy, and is *shared*. I said it was God that was evident after we all learned that I had been healed, and, of course, it was, but the occasion demanded a different name. Jesus Christ.

Chris

MAY 2

Dear Chris,

This letter-writing of ours is like an exploratory hike without a map or a clear goal, on which, following a path, we come to many trailheads. On some we detour briefly and return to the original trail, which is right now turning to be about God. A wonderful thing about our hike is that we can return to trails not taken, that we *will* return to them—*Deo volente*, as some timid voice inside wants me to add. Having this unstructured correspondence with you is so refreshing (and so unlike our actual walks, always the same rectangular route: right on Canner, right on Orange, right on Chapel, right on Temple . . . which makes the meandering conversation possible). Sometimes it feels as if we are hiking on the same mountain and in the same direction, but on two trails in close proximity that keep merging and diverging. I love this conversation. I love observing how well you see and describe what you see. I love how disagreeing with you feels like disagreeing with myself, free of any envy and malice, which is how Augustine describes disagreement among friends.

When you mentioned "arguing," I thought immediately: This correspondence is not an argument to be won or lost. Do you think we are arguing? We are trying to understand each other—to articulate and make plausible, to a degree, our experiences with God, Christ, faith, and the lack of it. Such experiences have convictions about their "objects" embedded in them and therefore, if we take them seriously, invite something like arguments. You help me move toward clarity.

Now, none of this could we do if you and I just *were* nature, as Rilke might have it. I like the eighth of *The Duino Elegies* and will return to it in a moment, which I couldn't possibly do if what Rilke describes in such an austerely beautiful way were true, because then he couldn't have written it and I couldn't have read it. I am not suggesting that we are outside nature either, human animals as we are. We are a special kind of nature: nature capable of consciously *relating to* itself and to others. This conviction is not, I think, some residue of religiously motivated human exceptionalism or idealism of bygone times. Our colleague Martin Hägglund, an avowed atheist, affirms it resolutely as well in his most recent book, *This Life*. Maybe that's also what you assume when you insist on "craving for reality," in contrast to Rilke's flowers endlessly opening into pure space. In the language of Genesis: Human beings belong to the community of creatures as *bearers of God's image*. This distinction between human beings and the rest of the creation is no ontological divide, though. Together with everything that isn't God, we are on one side of the ontological divide. God is on the other. Alone—and yet most intimately present with each creature.

The fact that we consciously relate to nature is our curse. Rilke got that right. In the Genesis story of the forbidden tree—here again I invoke the Bible, without having responded to your damning accusation against the vileness of the holy book—Eve could not have been tempted without the ability to regulate her relation to the fateful tree through deliberation: "Hm? Did God really say that we should not eat from the tree of the knowledge of good and evil whose fruit is so obviously good and beautiful? Could a good God have meant it so literally?" Eve deliberates and, in the name of God's goodness, takes and eats (which is how Dietrich Bonhoeffer reads this story in his *Creation and Fall*).

But the fact that we relate to nature is our blessing as well. Rilke pushes against this. Would the Open be *the Open* if we couldn't at least for a moment step out of our unity with nature and come to know that which is before our eyes *as* the Open? And wouldn't it be a loss if we couldn't thematize that into which we open, if we couldn't experience it *as* mystery, couldn't know good *as* good? Rilke seems to romanticize the child. I am able to wish myself into that state, into living in the pure present, but only for a moment. Would not the innocence Rilke was perhaps after be stupefied—as Hegel puts it in his *Lectures on the Philosophy of Religion*—if it were devoid of consciousnesses and will? Union with God and with the world, though beyond words, is also a state of consciously being in the good—or in union with the Good—not a state of mere "natural" openness.

I might be making too much of the difference between "being nature" and "relating to nature," but the issue has bearing on how we think about God and relate to God. My impression is that, for you, "God" is associated with a certain dimension of our experiences, those we sometimes have and those after which we crave; God is the Inexpressible residing in these experiences, that which "appears" beyond the edges of the meaning-conveying words, in their untamed excess. If so, it would make sense that poetry, seeking as it often does to expand the boundaries of the sayable, brings you into contact with an *other* and has made you a lover of God. The movement of your faith seems mainly from experiences through the strain of language and into the Open, into that which all humans call God, to use the phrase with which Thomas Aquinas concludes each of his five "demonstrations" of God's existence. I am not suggesting that you, too, are offering an argument for the existence of God. You give the inexpressible in the experiences the name "God"—that is "what *a poet* would call God"—with an implicit invitation to others to see whether that resonates with their own experiences, and, for those who are Christians, whether that comports with who they understand God to be.

That's how I read *My Bright Abyss*, the best exemplar of this kind of account of faith's genesis that I know. Here is how I think of it (though I am not sure whether it bears any semblance to what you take yourself to be doing). As a poet, you fail gloriously—gloriously, because to succeed as a poet is to bring language to the point where it can *fail well*, where it is, like Rilke's flower, opening into pure space. As a human, though, you refuse to stay with this failure, longing for more than poetry can deliver. That refusal creates space for God to appear, and for the believer in you to be born. A surplus of experience brings faith into existence, not a discomfort with some absence, as in the God-of-the-gaps accounts of religion.

And yet, the availability of the space for God to appear does not itself make God appear (by which I mean that the excess of experience is not an *indication* that the experience is of God or of God at work). It is possible to accept the failure of language, to think that this is simply the way things are, and then the space for God to appear disappears. What legitimizes giving the Open the name God, which Rilke, a poet, does without warning? Must one not presuppose God to find God or the effects of God's agency in the Open? Unless the Open just *is* God, which is what Rilke might be implying. But neither you nor I would want to say *that*, I assume. The abyss might then turn out to be at times bright and at times very dark, and not in a good way.

My way of connecting God and experience of the world is more prosaic than what I understand to be yours, and it moves in the opposite direction, not from experience to God but from God to experience. In *The Varieties of Religious Experience*, William James suggests that the effect of a conversion on the convert's experience of the world is analogous to falling in love. Love, he writes, "transforms the value of the creature loved as utterly as the sunrise transforms Mont Blanc from a corpselike gray to a rosy enchantment." He gives many examples of conversions altering the converts' experiences of the world. One of the converts, Jonathan Edwards—yes, *the* Jonathan Edwards of the angry God—reports: "The appearance of everything was altered; there seemed to be, as it were, a calm, sweet cast, or appearance of divine glory, in almost everything." My own "falling in love" with God was more muted than the conversions of people in James's report; there was, in fact, no "falling," but only a gradual deepening of something like gratitude to God. For me, too, however, the main effect of faith in God is to see and experience the world differently, as a gift, first some narrow segments of it and then the world as a whole. This rescued the world from being a mere thing—in many regards a beautiful mere thing—and made it into a medium of relationship. The world became a bit like the drawing my five-year-old daughter surreptitiously slipped under my office door one evening when she should have been asleep but was in fact thinking of me; I can still hear the piece of paper scraping the floor and the quick tiptoed steps receding.

In moving from God to the experience of the world, I have to assume that God exists apart from the world and stands in a particular relationship to the world—that God created all that is (though not by some punctiliar act at an impossible beginning before time, but by abidingly bringing the world into existence *ex nihilo* and holding it together). God is then not just the condition of possibility of there being anything to experience and anyone to experience it. God makes the entirety of what is a gift to each created entity. "I believe that God has made me and all creatures; that He has given me my body and soul, eyes, ears . . ." writes Martin Luther in his *Small Catechism*, a basic manual for instruction in faith. Any and every person can, with equal legitimacy, say the same thing; in fact, the best way to say it is *together*, in each other's hearing.

Two kinds of movements. Each has to assume God, though the first motivates the assumption by pointing to the extraordinariness of the ordinary. In both, the world shimmers because of God; in the first, God appears *in* the world's shimmering and shining, and in the second, God *makes* the world shimmer and shine and makes one see it shimmer and shine. The beauty of it is that the two are not mutually exclusive. One could make the journey from the experiences to God and then from God back to a new way of having those same experiences. I meet my newborn child for the first time, and the experience bursts through the language into the Open; I recognize that into which the experience has burst as God. God "creates" the newborn, the One Jesus called his Father, the Giver of all good gifts, and this sense of God at work, in turn, elicits gratitude and deepens the joy over my newborn child. Perhaps both you and I combine the two movements, each in our own way.

The directionality of each of these "movements" raises a question I have wanted to ask you for some time. Do you think that people's experiences of the world, including religious experiences, are the same across cultures, but that people name them and frame them in linguistically and culturally distinct ways? Or, do you think that the culturally—and religiously—specific frames and ways of speaking with which we operate co-constitute concrete experiences, making them into what they are for us?

I intended to write about idolatry, that stubborn distortion of faith. Your "Nothing" in response to the question about what to do about our propensity to create false gods did what I think you intended it to do. It startled me. Though it turns out that the kind of nothing you have in mind is in fact a something. Let's put idolatry, along with God's absence, on our list of short trails that need exploring. What else should be on that list? Not Christ, who needs his own and long trail. Maybe death, which is hovering over our conversation, but is never explicitly thematized. (Close to death, does one look at death, or does one "stare *out*," as Rilke writes?) Mortality may end up a major trail as well, especially if we tie it to natality, that wonderful counterpoint Hannah Arendt made to Martin Heidegger's being-toward death. I just received Jennifer Banks's *Natality* and see that you endorsed it.

One final comment, fitting, I think, because this entire letter has Rilke's eighth elegy as background. I am rereading Bonhoeffer's *Letters and Papers from Prison*, and last night I read a letter written to his close friend Eberhard Bethge, in which Bonhoeffer complains that his fiancée, Maria von Wedemeyer, loves Rilke, whereas he finds Rilke "outright unhealthy." Bonhoeffer is troubled about her taste in poetry and is half-confessing a "tyrannical" urge to bring her in alignment with his views. Not our problem. I am not nearly as displeased with Rilke as Bonhoeffer was, and you seem less wedded to him than Dietrich makes Maria to be.

Miroslav

MAY 13

Dear Miroslav,

Do you really believe that—that all life is one side of a divide, and God is alone on the other? It seems such a sad vision, for us as well as for God. And how does Christ figure into this relationship? If Christ is God, then God is clearly on the other side of the partition as well. I anticipate you will say it is only an ontological distinction, that God is *in* our side of the partition (your daughter dropping her note) but not *of* it, that he is both immanent and transcendent. This I can get behind, but it's hardly as separate as that partition implies.

You mention Luther so often that I decided to read him. I remember you telling me on a walk once that Marilynne Robinson considers *The Freedom of a Christian* to be the supreme achievement of Western prose, which seems to me . . . odd. It's sharp and cunning, and I love the bitchy intro in which he pretends only to want to save the noble pope from the vipers that surround him. But it's hardly *that* memorable as a piece of writing. Robinson herself has written more indelible prose.

And this endless emphasis on *faith*. Of course, Luther had

his reasons for it, but it's been a baleful influence on Christianity, which has become far too removed from its origins in Judaism (which is, of course, what Luther wanted). My undergraduate Jewish students always tell me that Judaism isn't interested in faith, that the question simply doesn't come up. My reading of Soloveitchik, Heschel, and even Martin Buber and Gershom Scholem makes me doubt this clean distinction, but I take the point. There is not this inner, intimate necessity, this constant and accusatory compulsion, at the center of Judaism. And it is freer—*truer*—for it.

This goes to your question about whether humans share certain spiritual experiences or whether we have those experiences because of culture. Do I experience the anguish of faith because it's simply my nature (and shared by countless others of different traditions), or do I suffer from a seed of anxiety that was planted in me by a very nervous church in my childhood? Both, probably. If I hadn't been raised a Christian, I suspect I would still have a strong hunger for God and would be buffeted by erratic storms of love and lack. (Some of my Jewish students certainly experience this.) But I wouldn't define it as some internal action called faith, wouldn't berate myself for not having it. Faith is a gift, not a capacity. Christians—especially Protestants—have too often made it seem the latter. Do you see what I mean here? Do you agree?

Interestingly, yesterday I was in Cambridge and had another cup of tea with Fanny Howe. She told me that she sometimes decides to be an atheist for a week. She does this because she admires atheism, the purity of it (obviously she's not talking about the insipid forms of "neo-atheism" that have been so conspicuous in American culture recently), and because it seems to her part of the experience of God. That's what Weil thought ("There are two atheisms of which one is a purification of God") and it's what I have been saying in a different way in some of these letters. But still, I found myself baffled. I could no more "decide" to not believe in God than I could decide to believe in him. Sometimes I find myself having fallen into atheism, though it is in no way purifying. It feels like failure, spiritual torpor, acedia. My point is that I don't feel in control of my belief in this way. I am in control of my *attention*, and that matters enormously, but whatever ignites attention into faith, whatever makes my seeing reciprocal, that is beyond me.

One more addendum/digression: It's not poetry's capacity

for reaching into the unsayable that readied me for God, or at least not only, or even primarily, that. It's a couple of other things. First, the mystery of poetry (and other arts, I expect) is that in moments of true inspiration one isn't simply looking but being seen. That's what I mean by reciprocal seeing. It's as if reality looks back at you, and for me that gaze is God's. And second, I feel completely estranged from my best poems; they are cold as moonstones to me. I have little memory of writing them (making specific decisions, I mean, pondering alternatives, that kind of thing) and feel no pride for them. It's as if something moved through me and made the poem. I suppose that sounds like hubris—me as some blessed vessel—but what I feel is profound humility. It's that feeling of having been erased for the sake of something greater, of bringing forth something so far beyond my own capacities, that first led me to think the word *faith*.

I don't understand what you mean when you say that we couldn't be having this dialogue (which I agree is a gift) unless we were separate from nature. Unless you're simply saying that language itself is what separates us. But that's not true. Some species of animals do have language—whales can communicate great subtleties across immense distances—though, of course, not the complex arrangement of signs that humans have developed. But why should language define consciousness? The more we learn about animals, the less able we are to separate ourselves from them. (See Frans de Waal's *Are We Smart Enough to Know How Smart Animals Are?*) The more we learn about consciousness, the more evident it is that consciousness is a continuum, evident in animals, beyond question, but also possible in some rudimentary sense even in some flora. We may be at the pinnacle of consciousness (though I wouldn't bet on even this), but thinking of ourselves as separate from nature in this way seems to me not only wrong but dangerous. It is precisely why nature and our own souls are so degraded.

Rilke is actually making the same mistake in the eighth Duino Elegy. He's sentimentalizing nature as something beyond and apart from us. How can he possibly *know* that animals live in some perpetual present tense, that they are forever facing the Open and unburdened both by memory and imagination? A couple of years ago I had occasion to read some studies of rats being observed (tortured, really) for anxiety treatments. I'll spare you the details, but one upshot of the studies was that rats are capable of metacognition—that is, they know what they don't know. According to cognitive scientists, this is a chief criterion of consciousness. There are animals a lot smarter than rats. Who are we to say they don't fear death, need friends, taste grief simply because they don't write it down?

A thought experiment, not at all unlikely. Humans manage to wipe themselves out in one way or another, but some other species survive. The world ticks on timelessly. Where is God for this world and for these creatures?

What I think Rilke is *not* sentimentalizing is childhood, no more than Wordsworth was. There really is a "visionary gleam" to things that slowly fades into "the light of common day." Fanny Howe puts it like this:

> To resist the reality of time is to resist leaving childhood behind. [Simone Weil] called this resistance a flaw in herself, but is it? The self is not the soul, and it is the soul (coherence) that lives for nine years on earth in a potential state of liberty and harmony. Its openness to metamorphosis is usually sealed up during those early years until the self replaces the soul as the fist of survival.

You say, like Weil, that to persist in such an existence would leave one "stupefied." I'm not so sure. Every (good) poet I know is in some way an adult child. They may be functioning as an ordinary adult (though some decidedly aren't), but there remains some primary permeability to them, some openness to nature (which includes humans!), and God (however defined), and radical change. Of course, it's not a constant state. That would be madness, which sadly does claim a high percentage of poets. That's probably what you're suggesting. But I doubt Rilke believed we could attain the state of consciousness he describes, except in flashes—and even then available only for the aristocrats among us. Rilke was a snob.

We're still talking primarily of God and not Christ. Fanny said another arresting thing yesterday. She said she often felt she was more of a Jew than a Christian because she is obsessed with God and spends her days pondering him, but it requires a real effort to turn her attention to Christ. I realized this is true of me as well, and that I don't want it to be true, because without the incarnation I don't understand the universal communion of all reality that is probably my most settled belief; and without the crucifixion I don't understand suffering. So this is a direction in which we must turn, and soon, but before that I have three questions for you that are burning a hole in the pocket of my mind, as it were.

First, what place does the Bible have in your religious life? You base your belief on the separation of humans from nature on the verse saying we are created in God's image. But the Bible also says that God is aware of every blade of grass and feels every sparrow's fall. Nor is there a word for "nature" in the Bible, which suggests no line between us and it (no "it"). How do you decide what parts of the Bible to believe? Because some of it, let's face it, is whacko. Luther said the Bible actually wasn't the Word of God until it was read in the light of the Holy Spirit, which seems to me squarely in line with my own notion that each creates his own version of God (Luther's spinning in his crypt), because who gets to determine which interpretations are inspired?

Second, I really want to know how you interpret Christ's resurrection in light of the Trinity. You said a couple of letters back that it was not the case that the first person (God) raised the second person (Jesus), but that is exactly what Paul said happened. Predictably, I'm not troubled by Paul's comments because I think Paul was often wrong (no women babbling in church!). But I'm really interested in hearing how you reconcile your belief with these verses and, even more so, in how Jesus can be both God and not.

And third, I'm still dying to hear about your feeling for God's absence! Specifically, did something change between your comment to me in class about never having felt God's absence and the feeling of "motherlessness" you described in one of our earliest letters?

Chris

MAY 25

Dear Chris,

If I wait any longer to write about God's absence, it will seem like I am avoiding the issue; I myself will start suspecting it. I am glad I have waited, though. For we seem to have come closer on an issue that is decisive for how I think about God's absence: the nature of the relation between God and the world.

A divide between God and the world, even a separation between the two, was from the beginning your major concern with my understanding of God. I, in turn, was uneasy with what I perceived as a merger of the two, approaching even to God's dependence on humans for existence. This divergence between us was first on the list of concerns and questions in your last letter. And yet, it looks like we are not far apart. If you affirm the *ontological* divide between God and creation, then we differ largely only in language and emphasis. We are both against the separation of the two in reality. I've written a whole book arguing that God's coming to dwell in creation, to make it the home of all creatures and be at home in it, is what God created the world for. This is what happens decisively and, according to the Christian tradition, uniquely in the particularity of the human body of Jesus Christ, the fully human and fully divine One.

For me, as for many theologians, the ontological divide between God and the world does not imply separation at all; to the contrary, it makes God's most intimate union with creatures possible. Rowan Williams and our colleague Kathryn Tanner make this point powerfully. On our side of the ontological divide, if two entities want to occupy the same space, they will jostle with each other for that space. If one wins, the other will lose. Not so with God and a creature. God can be inside me without having pushed any of me out; God can irradiate me from within into a liveliness that is properly my own and yet God's doing—and a liveliness in which I both act and do not "achieve" the result. This is how Luther describes God's presence in human lives in *The Freedom of a Christian*. I see some affinity between your experience of writing poetry and such divine irradiation of the self: Something moves through you when you write; you have written your best poems, but there is "no pride" for the result. But when you describe your experience, God and you seem exclusive alternatives, as if in this process there is no room for both God and you; "something" other than you "made the poem." At the level of experience, this surely feels right. But at the deeper level, this must be wrong, both in your writing of poetry and in God's coming to dwell in creatures. For Luther, as for many Christian theologians before and after him, both God and humans are active at the same time. To use an ancient metaphor, the relation between God and the self is like that of heat and an iron that has sat in fire; the iron is glowing hot on account of the source of heat outside of it, and yet the heat is also the iron's.

In Genesis, a noncompetitive kind of relation between God and humans is constitutive of our humanity itself, and not merely of our agency as humans: God breathes God's breath into Adam and thereby makes him human. Echoing the story of Adam's creation, the Psalmist says something similar of sparrows and blades of grass:

> When You hide your face, they panic,
>   You withdraw their breath and they perish
>   and to the dust they return.
> When You send forth Your breath, they are created,
>   and You renew the face of the earth.

The presence of God in the very fabric of a creature translates existentially into a certain kind of awareness of God's presence at all times. In one of my favorite Psalms, we read:

> Where can I go from Your spirit,
>   And where from before You flee?
> If I soar to the heavens, You are there,
>   if I bed down in Sheol—there You are.
> If I take wing with the dawn,
>   if I dwell at the ends of the sea,
> there, too, Your hand leads me,
>   and Your right hand seizes me.
> Should I say, "Yes, darkness will swathe me,
>   and the night will be light for me,"
> darkness itself will not darken for You,
>   and the night will light up like the day,
>   the dark and the light will be one.

Because of the ontological divide, God can be closer to creatures than they are to themselves—to borrow a phrase from Augustine that strikes me as substantively a bit off but rhetorically correct. *Because* of the ontological divide, there is existential inseparability: God is always everywhere the creature goes. All of this has bearing on the problem of God's absence.

I am mostly in a state of faith—it is a strange phrase, "state of faith"; more common is "state of grace," but I think that we are all always in the state of grace—but sometimes I fall out of a state of faith, often when I am struck by the absurdity of life or troubled by the rivers of tears and blood with which history, like the lacerated and pierced body of the crucified Christ, bleeds. At those times, doubt does not, as usual, just grumble under its breath against the faith that is in charge but rises up to pull faith down from its throne. Like a chimera, God then disappears into nothingness. You might think that I would feel distress at God's absence. I don't, and I don't fully understand why, given how much God means to me. I do feel distress in that state, but not over God's absence, perhaps because such distress would presume that God could and should be present and make a difference. With God gone, the "should" of God's existence and help is gone, too. In my unbelief, God is not far. God is not idle. God just isn't. My distress is a sense of cosmic motherlessness. I don't just *feel* motherless. I *am* a motherless person who would like to have had a mother but never did and never will. I am alone, with a friend or two, in my little boat on the open sea. The friends are mostly good company, which is something. But they are as helpless as I am against the terror of the raging sea. No God is sleeping on a cushion in our boat that is about to be swamped. Nobody I could wake up to rebuke the wind and say to the waves: "Peace! Be still!" Sometimes I wish I could be a fatalist, as was my uncle during the war in Croatia in the 1990s. When Osijek, the town in which he lived and in which I was born, was under artillery fire, he would stand on the balcony of his fourth floor apartment and observe the spectacle. If a projectile had his name on it, it would find him wherever he was.

Though it seems at times and for a while to be dead, a dethroned faith is not dead, at least in my case. Unbelief's naysaying has to keep my faith from rising up, and for my unbelief to stay alive, it needs to feed on faith. I have never come into the kind of unbelief in which the negation of God would be unnecessary, like the ideal case of atheism for Karl Marx, in which God never even comes to mind so as to become an object of negation. Dethroned faith is not entirely passive. It whispers into unbelief's ears the tales of life's possibilities and often turns doubt against itself: doubt doubting doubt. More important than this occasional self-undermining of doubt is the discovery that I make again and again: Even when God disappears for me, I don't disappear for God; when I have no faith in God, God still has faith in me and remains faithful.

In *The Invention of Religion*, an extraordinary book about the story of Exodus, Jan Assmann suggests that after years of slavery and exploitation, the Israelites had actually forgotten God. When they "groaned under their slavery, and cried out," they were not crying out *to* God but just crying out in pain and despair. Though not directed to God, their cry "rose up to God": "God heard their groaning, and God remembered his covenant with Abraham, Isaac, and Jacob. God looked upon the Israelites, and God took notice of them." Unbidden, God comes to the rescue, though the puzzlement remains that God showed up, according to the narrative, only after 430 years of exile and much cruel abuse.

That's my experience of God's absence and God's arrival when I am in the state of doubt. When I am in a state of faith, God's absence from me, understood literally, is ruled out. As long as I am, I know that God is present to me. If God were not, I would not be. As a believer, I use the language of absence not to designate the "departure" of the God who ought to be with me, but the failure of God to do what I think is right to expect

God to do. I haven't done a careful study of God's "absence" in the Bible—there I go again, back to the book you are tempted to call unholy—but in many cases that's what absence means there, too. When a devout person cries to God in Psalm 22, "My God, my God, why have you forsaken me?" they don't mean "Why are you not here spatially?" but "Why are you sitting on your divine hands with your mouth shut when I need you the most? Either do something or explain yourself!" Similarly, when the question appears in the mouth of the mockers in Psalm 42, "Where is your God?" they don't mean primarily "Why is God not present?" but "Why is the God whom you trust not intervening when you are crumbling under the onslaught of the enemy?" It is significant that the Gospels read Jesus's experience on the cross with the help of both of these Psalms.

Though God is never absent, I often *feel* that God is absent, most palpably, in fact, when I pray, as I mentioned earlier: The words start their journey on sound waves and quickly dissipate into airy nothingness. I know that God is not absent, but in my experience, the "space" that God should occupy is empty. I don't have a need to *feel* God's presence. I don't write this with the smugness of an enlightened theologian: We who know who God is and how God is, we know that God isn't an object in the world and therefore cannot be felt. I am not actually sure that the inference is right, that God cannot make it that humans can feel God and that God does not feel. I always admired my mother for having a very intimate, though often difficult, friendship with God. She told me that it took her years and long hours in prayer to begin to feel God's presence and to come to hear God speak, and that even after she had learned to feel and hear God, she sometimes had to wait longingly for God to show up and, when God showed up, to hear God speak. In the times of waiting, she did not think that God was absent and could not hear her, but that God was not there *for her*. A bit like her husband, on whom she knew she could always rely but who was often emotionally unavailable to her, even when he was sitting right next to her and listening to her.

I don't have the experiences with God that my mother had, though I wish I did. Still, looking back at my life, I don't think that God was ever absent, that God was ever not doing what God was supposed to do. Maybe that's because I have not suffered enough, not looked death in the face as you have. (But then, the seas have not always been calm for me either.) Maybe that's because I have not been fully existentially invested in people or projects to be utterly devastated when failure or loss came. (But then, I cannot imagine loving more some people I have lost.) Maybe that's because my expectations of God were too low to be disappointed. (But then, everything I have I experience as God's gift, and I can easily imagine God giving me more and better gifts.) Maybe some rosy spectacles are permanently fixed on my face, like the green ones everyone received before entering Oz's Emerald City. (But then, given how self-aggrandizing evil is and how horizon-defining is even its mere prospect, what exactly does it mean to give both the good and the evil their proper due in memory and attention?)

Early on in my life, it was seared into my soul that, God or no God, losses, sometimes horrendous, will come. By the time I was born my mother had given birth to four children, three of whom tragically died; a child that came into the world after me was stillborn. Our lives are not in our control, and whoever controls them rarely seems to have our best interests in mind. If I don't hold lightly things that are very dear to me, in losing them I will also lose myself, a point Kierkegaard elaborates in *Either/Or* by retelling the story of Margarete and Faust. And even before I myself am lost, without such lightness much of my love itself would be tarnished and twisted. I can never love rightly the things that I hold too tightly for the fear of losing them, because then, while I still have them, my love will be too grasping and self-undermining. (The adverb "lightly" is inadequate, but I am not coming up with a better one. In *Letters and Papers from Prison*, Bonhoeffer struggles with the issue and opts for "detachment," which I think is dead wrong. I am looking for a word that would signal two attitudes at the same time: "I'll do anything for you!" and "If I were to lose you, I'd be deeply wounded but not destroyed." My relation to the object of my love is not unmediated attachment and fusion; it is mediated in part through will. I am fumbling to express a human analogue to the divine kind of love: unconditionally invested and generous, but not dependent.)

Though I have never been able to trust the world fully, I have come to trust God, for the most part. That trust is not an inference from the trustworthiness of the world to its transcendent cause, but an existential wager on the primacy of goodness, the world's untrustworthiness notwithstanding. I trust God even when God isn't doing what seems reasonable to think that God should do. While insisting that God is love, unconditional and unalterable, I accept that I don't know what it is that I have the right to expect from God. That's what I find in the book of Job.

In an earlier letter, you wrote, tersely and powerfully as only you can, that the book of Job "enacts, rather than explains, the shock of God." Some interpreters—you are among them, if I am not mistaken—think that if we read the body of the book together with its introduction and conclusion, the happy ending cushions conveniently the shock. (I leave aside here the question of whether Job's recompense at the end is too naive, and whether Job's first family appear in it, as you put it, simply as "collateral casualties for Job's illumination.") As I see it, the book has a happy ending, but with a crucial and deeply disconcerting twist. The ending seems to match the beginning, with a surplus, as if his righteousness were part of some commodity exchange: Money→Commodity [tested righteousness]→Money', where the prime stands for increased return. But that's not quite right. For part of his illumination is the realization that the ordeal can happen again any moment despite anything he does. (I found this reading of Job's ending first in an unpublished essay by Sameer Yadav and then later saw that Rowan Williams had suggested it in *The Tragic Imagination*.) Written with only the one ordeal in view, the book, without bookends, *is* a scream and a prayer, as you put it, or, with its bookends, might be read to offer a cheap consolation. But how would a sequel be written if the second ordeal were to happen—after Job has had all his arguments with

God, after God has made the speech from the whirlwind, after he had seen God and acknowledged his own nonunderstanding? That's the disturbing question with which the book leaves me. It occurred to me that, perhaps, we have an answer in the way the crucifixion of Jesus is rendered in the New Testament.

After the countless ordeals of history—my own are negligible and almost beside the point—I am left with two options. I can recognize soberly that there is no God who could calm the storm, and that cursing God in misplaced anger would only implicitly affirm the existence of the One who just isn't. Or, I can make a wager on God and the primacy of goodness, while knowing that the ways of God with the world are enveloped in darkness. With Job, I embrace this second option. I trust God, notwithstanding, without expectation that God will do otherwise than God actually does and therefore without experiencing God's absence. Still, I do hope that our colleague and my good friend Keith DeRose will succeed in showing that the slaughter bench of history and God's goodness are somehow compatible, that one can actually narrate God's defeat of evil. Even if he does, the wager of trust will still be necessary. My trust is not based on the conviction that "everything happens for a reason" but, to match this worn-out phrase with another one, that "God knows how to write straight even on crooked lines."

Since I am writing about trust, a digression about "faith," to address one of your concerns in the last letter: When Luther says, in *The Freedom of a Christian*, "If you believe, you shall have all things," a claim about faith which troubles you in this text, "believing" doesn't mean primarily "holding some claims about God to be true," although that is involved, too, but, above all, "entrusting your life to God." In his *Lectures on Galatians*, Luther likens faith to the prongs on a ring that hold the diamond, which is Christ. For him, faith or believing is always an existential act and never a mere doxastic attitude. The second part of that treatise is all about love, which trust in God and holding Christ make possible. The whole treatise is about love, I think, answering the question of how one comes to love with the right kind of love.

Because I trust God, I also hope in God. Hope is trust on its tiptoes, said Charlie Moule, a Cambridge New Testament scholar of the previous generation, whom I read as a teenager. In the course of living out the wager of trust, I have come to believe, mainly under the influence of Moltmann's *Theology of Hope*, that hope isn't a reasonable expectation that some determinate positive goal, the hope's object, will become reality. Instead—and this, too, comes from Luther—hope is a way of living into the future with objects of expectation themselves only vaguely and tentatively known. And lightly held, too, with a readiness to recognize as the hope's fulfillment even things that weren't explicit in expectation. In *Lectures on Romans*, Luther puts concretely what I have just stated abstractly: Hope, he writes, transfers a person "into the unknown, the hidden, and the dark shadow, so that he does not even know what he hopes for." And then, miracle of miracles, in the arrival of that which was beforehand not known or not fully known, I recognize with joy the object of my hope! The paradigmatic case of such an arrival is the advent of Christ as the Gospels narrate it. He both fulfilled and transformed hopes. Does any of this make sense?

Before I sign off, I should comment briefly about another separation that you see in my letters, the one between humans and animals (which, some would wrongly claim, is of a piece with the separation between God and the world). I, too, reject that separation but affirm the distinction. Biologically, humans are animals; theologically, they are creatures and belong to the community of creation. I don't deny the consciousness or intelligence of other animals. How could I, given how smart my favorite creature, the octopus, is?! But I take it that no octopus, elephant, or pig (to name two more very smart animals) asks itself "What *should* I do?" and "Who *should* I be?" Because I ask these questions, I can read Rilke and Nietzsche, worry about my life in light of their thought, and possibly change its direction or insist that one or the other is mistaken. That is what I meant by the claim that humans are "nature that consciously relates to itself and others."

Miroslav

PS. I would really like to know how you think about idolatry. What is it? How much do you worry about it? In a future letter I will respond to your comments about Luther's *The Freedom of a Christian*. The worst of Luther—his frequent bitchiness—is just about the best he does in the text, I hear you saying. I feel obliged, by my respect for Luther and Marilynne Robinson, to respond to the provocation!

JUNE 12

Dear Miroslav,

I didn't know we shared an affinity for the octopus. In Sy Montgomery's book about the octopus, she describes being taken by the hand and very carefully guided to an octopus's lair as if to a home showing, then taken on a tour of the more interesting places of the reef where it lived. I'd say this is a creature that probably does ask itself "What should I do," and I wouldn't want to bet against it asking "Who should I be?" Though I still don't find those questions determinative of consciousness or selfhood, and certainly not closeness to God. At the end of her book, Montgomery says, "If I have a soul—and I think I do—I am sure the octopus has one as well."

There are roughly 8.7 million classified species in the world. Scientists estimate that there remain 5 million that have not been discovered. Include microbes and bacteria, and that number jumps to a trillion. Who knows what these creatures at the bottom of the ocean or in the as-yet-undestroyed reaches of the forests are thinking or not thinking? Who knows what part they play in the unity of the universe? One thing is certain, though, they exist in relation to their creator before they have anything to do with us. (I'm watering down Rowan Williams's brilliant thoughts on this subject.) Christianity has to outgrow its notion that the universe is a theater in which we are the stars. We may very well, with nuclear war or environmental catastrophe or some insidious AI, wipe ourselves off the face of the planet. And the world will go on working, and some resilient creatures will go on with their enigmatic lives, and God will be there for and in them.

> I do not understand; but I believe.
> Jonquils respond with wit to the teasing breeze.
>
> —John Berryman, "Eleven
> Addresses to the Lord"

Perhaps one thing I am coming around to saying is that it's a mistake to always read nature through scripture. The "book of nature" precedes the Good Book, after all, and we might do well to use it as a lens to clarify the latter. For instance, I have wondered (and still wonder) how you explain the crucifixion of Christ, how God could be in two places at once without being two gods. Quantum physics suggests a way of reading that event. Just as position and momentum split under observation, so that we can never know both at the same time, perhaps our perception of God at the moment of the crucifixion and resurrection depends upon our focus. Look one way, and God is a noun (position), crucified on Golgotha and entirely dead. Look another way and he is a verb (momentum), an unceasing energy that can wrest life from nothingness. And just as with physical reality, each manifestation of God is an absolute truth, or, if you prefer (and I do), a relative truth that we experience absolutely.

We are still some way from each other with regard to the absence of God. You see it as a perception of absence, a failure on the individual's part (if I am reading you correctly). I see it as a reality—God died on the cross, and at times in our lives, and in the life of a culture, he is equally absent. This has nothing to do with circumstance, or at least is not determined by it. I have felt close to God in the midst of great physical suffering. But we—by which I mean we modern people—are not simply "wrong" when we perceive the absolute absence of God in our time. When Bonhoeffer says we are called to live in a world without God, or when Simone Weil says that absence is the form God's presence takes for us now, or when Marilynne Robinson shows the soul's loneliness to be a natural phenomenon as real and ineluctable as gravity (I'm thinking of *Housekeeping*, a book that does seem to read scripture through nature)—all are expressing not a failure of consciousness but a kind of culmination. Part of God's reality is unreality, in that it is forever beyond our perception. This need not lead to despair (though Lord knows it can). "Sumptuous destitution" is the provocative phrase of Dickinson's, and all of the writers I just mentioned are attuned to the volatile goneness of God. But he is not in abeyance, so to speak, not waiting in the wings for us to turn and recognize him. God is dead. God is our salvation. God is a noun. God is a verb. But I'm not sure we can know the truth of one without knowing the truth of the other.

Which leads me to your question about idolatry. It has occurred to me—how could it not?—that my emphasis on the absence of God may be a form of idolatry.

> Try to remember this: what you project
> Is what you will perceive; what you perceive
> With any passion, be it love or terror,
> May take on whims and powers of its own.
>
> —Richard Wilbur, "Walking to Sleep"

I try to be aware of this—my last book's subtitle was, after all, "Fifty Entries Against Despair"—and try to cleave to the hope you articulate so well. (Moltmann says hope is what faith matures into.) But God's absence has been, both in my own life and in the lives of so many famished souls of the past century and a half—too obdurate and implacable a fact to wish away as a matter of perceptual limitation.

In any event, the issue of religious idolatry is more interesting and immediate to me than other forms. Money, fame, power, the circumscription and exaltation of the self—these are the old bugbears, obvious and easily identified (but how hard to kill!). But when God himself becomes an idol, that's when the issue becomes especially prickly and difficult to disentangle. After a talk I gave at a divinity school some years ago, a well-known theologian came up to me and offered, not kindly, to instruct me in theology so that I wouldn't continue to disfigure God. I felt like a medical intern being reprimanded for putting the patient in danger. In the twenty years (!) that I have been writing and thinking more directly about theological concerns, I have encountered this form of intellectual idolatry often. Theology is a lot like poetry in that it requires a renewable innocence. Implicit in the most powerful and convincing theology one hears a whisper, *I don't know*. (It will embarrass you, but I think of you as a model in this regard.) The theologian protecting her province (and God!) from me, the conservative public figures proof-texting scripture to justify their cruelties, the liberal leaders warping the Bible to accommodate contemporary social concerns, my own inclination to make God and art one thing—idolatries, all.

Every statement about God is provisional (including this one). On our last walk we talked some of Gianni Vattimo and his theory that nihilism is the ultimate expression of Christ's life and message. I find this more provocative and helpful than you do, though I do think "nihilism" is the wrong word (love survives in Vattimo's schema), and I don't really think that nihilism is the final fruition of Christ and his message, because there is no "final" fruition to be had. But to think of Christ as the "great unmasker," as Vattimo puts it, to think of his life as God's complete assent to the incarnation, that is, to be completely material—might not this be seen as a development of Bonhoeffer's ideas of a religionless Christianity? Bonhoeffer didn't want to do away with the church—he was an orthodox Lutheran pastor, for goodness' sake. It was *metaphysics* that Bonhoeffer wanted to be freed from—in essence, it was that wholly internal movement of "faith" that Luther described and demanded. As Bonhoeffer writes,

> God would have us know that we must live as men who manage our lives without him. The god who is with us is the god who forsakes us. The God who lets us live in the world without the working hypothesis of God is the God before whom we stand continually. Before God and with God we live without God. God lets himself be pushed out of the world on to the cross. He is weak and powerless in the world, and that is precisely the way, *the only way*, in which he is with us and helps us. (Italics mine!)

Sometimes I wonder, Miroslav, if my very obsession with God is an idol, if life is not meant to be this single-minded chase. Maybe grace, for some, is God forgotten.

But that's not the note I want to end on. No, I have had two experiences recently that make all this *thought* about God seem like so much guff. Or do they actually confirm it? You be the judge.

Last week I went to New York for a few days to reconnect with an old friend, who flew in from Chicago. We have both had tempests in our lives of late, and we are both deeply committed to God, so our conversations were focused and stimulating and consoling. One afternoon we were seated at a café on the Upper West Side discussing, coincidentally, Bonhoeffer and his ideas about Christ. A homeless man kept edging up to the table trying to catch our eyes. I thought from the way my friend was positioned he couldn't see the man and, not wanting to interrupt the conversation, I kept my eyes scrupulously unfocused. The man edged this way and that before finally giving up and moving on. "Talking of Jesus while ignoring a beggar," my friend said immediately. I was so shocked that he was aware of the man that I lied and said I hadn't noticed him. How suddenly and wholly the vileness of our natures can make itself felt, saturating our selves like a drop of ink in clear water. Even telling the story here I shift to the general (*our!*), when what I felt at the moment (and have felt intensely since) was deep shame that extended to every limit of my being. And stopped there. I didn't include my friend; my self-saturation wouldn't let me. That man was *exactly* what Bonhoeffer meant by religionless Christianity—God in the world as not-God, Christ's life in us (or not) as love for others, not a whiff of metaphysics to it—and what Vattimo means by the persistence and possibility of love. I memorized the books and failed the test.

Then this: I had a follow-up PET scan in Boston a few days ago. For PET scans you are strapped onto a table so you won't move at all during the procedure. I often fall sound asleep (and sometimes twitch disastrously) but this time spent every minute in prayer. I prayed first for that man in New York and for forgiveness (which, of course, I had already done), and then I found myself praying for people in my life, sliding from one to another almost will-lessly, and then I found myself (again, I felt guided) simply praying without words, alert to God's presence—inextricable from his rational absence—in the whirring machine, the technician's voice, my own illuminated cells. Before God and with God we live without God? That sounds about right.

Chris

PS. I wasn't dismissing Luther's work in toto. I don't know it well enough to have a meaningful opinion about it. I was simply questioning the *literary* achievement of *The Freedom of a Christian* and only because Marilynne rates it so highly. (I assume she was reading it in English.) Luther would no doubt say that the whole question is, given the stakes and circumstances, irrelevant. And he would be right.

(By the way, I do realize that Luther was stressing the existential component in faith and not some doxastic alignment. *That* is what I am lamenting, that this internal action, which after all these centuries remains obscure—what, exactly, does it mean to "love" God? what does this internal assent *look like*?—has acquired such primacy and consequence in our lives. It does not feel like "freedom" to me.)

JULY 30

Dear Miroslav,

Should we let these letters go? I haven't heard from you in a long time. The one rule we had was that we could never complain about the other's silence, that the correspondence must never become a burden. I'm not violating that, I hope. But I miss you and also feel a sense of unease about what to do with all of these thoughts.

Danielle just came back from Mass and came straight upstairs to say to me, "I just have the feeling that we must not forget." I said, "I don't. I think about God constantly. He is essentially the entire content of my mind." She said, "No, no, that's not what I mean. I mean that we are living in the middle of a miracle."

It is so easy to forget. The crucible we have just passed through. *Are still passing through.* I feel the old imperative—work, work, work—closing in on me, not as a prompt to something new but merely sterile reproach. When all around me existence simply wants to sing.

I reviewed a good book, Michael Edwards's *The Bible and Poetry*. The real surprise of it was how much space he spends on the New Testament, where there isn't any poetry, strictly speaking, at least not original poetry. Edwards opens up some crucial passages ("This is my body," for instance) and makes a convincing (though, of course, I'm the choir here) case that most of "religion" is simply an error, irrelevant to the life of Christ and the lives he meant for us to lead. I have such a hunger for church—no, for *shared* prayer and praise—but have given up on having it fed.

I hope all is well with you, and that you and Jessica and Mira are having a peaceful summer away from school. We were in England and Tennessee and still have Texas and Maine ahead of us. It's a summer of travel, which I don't ordinarily relish, but it has been a good thing for our family.

Chris

AUGUST 8

Dear Chris,

This letter has been calling me for almost two months now, but I've only been able to respond with a version of a guilt-and-regret-laced "Just let me . . ." There was a lot of traveling and of traveling woes, but the blame falls on a stubborn cold (two months now and not yet over!) and a looming deadline for *The Cost of Ambition* book in which I have a chapter on Milton. (Reading what I wrote, I am sure today's Miltonists will have an analogous feeling to the one I have reading some of their texts: They just don't know enough theology to read Milton's two great poems well.) Our correspondence, its topics coursing through my mind day and night, was such an important part of my life this year. And there is so much to explore. After an unwilling break, I am glad to be back.

My attempt to enlist Milton as an ally in exposing the dark side of striving for superiority—I define it as striving to be better than others—reminded me that our little dispute about the place of humans in nature is largely about a matter of fact without much consequence for our conversation about faith. As for much of the Jewish and Christian traditions, for Milton, humans are not the only creatures who enjoy what, following Hägglund, I called spiritual freedom. In *Paradise Lost*, most of the actors are *angels*, and they are creatures with spiritual freedom, as the fall of some and the allegiance to God of others attests. If the octopus turns out to be more akin in this regard to angels and humans than to sea bass, all the better. What matters is spiritual freedom. Without it a creature could not make God an object of either love or hatred—or, for that matter, of indifference. Though God's relation to each creature is prior and more fundamental than a creature's relation to God. It secures their inherent dignity, as your reference to Rowan's comment suggests: None is created just for humans' sake, except in the sense in which all creatures, humans included, form a community of creation and are, in diverse ways, there for one another. But a creature's active relation to God—to the object of our ultimate trust and love—matters as well.

During my silence, Jessica and I went on a trip with a large group—some friends, mostly acquaintances—tracing part of St. Paul's journeys on a marvelous sailboat. I enjoyed it, maybe a bit too much; we were too pampered for the trip to help us identify with a man who was shipwrecked three times. During the fourteen-day trip, my mind returned often to our letters. You suggested that I read Fosse's *Septology*. I took it with me and read almost every word of its single sentence, more than 650 pages long. At times it seemed that Asle, the protagonist, had in his own head a very similar conversation to the one that you and I are having in this correspondence. I am eager to hear your take on Asle's experiences of God (on the relation of transcendence and immanence, for instance), of art (his "shining darkness" brought to mind your "bright abyss"), of consciousness (so many selves in a single self, those called Asle and those whose names are or contain permutations of the same letters!), of prayer (its rigidly liturgical and tactile form—often in Latin!—triggered by and spilling into inchoate ordinary awareness that it transforms into something like prayer), and more.

In Istanbul, we made sail for ancient Philippi, a place where, in 49 AD, the Christian faith arrived for the first time on the European continent. The ruins of Roman temples and ancient Christian churches—a floor mosaic in one of them with Paul's name in Greek letters—brought back to mind our differing assessments of Luther's *The Freedom of a Christian*, his little literary present to Pope Leo X, who excommunicated him, "the wild boar from the forest" destroying the Lord's vineyard. Sophia, a brilliant young archeologist, was our guide to first-century

Philippi, at the time a Roman colony. She organized the tour around the contrast between two political theologies and two "lords." In Roman political theology, there are many gods, but only one lord, the emperor. If you publicly, in acts of worship, recognize the sole lordship of the emperor, you can be a devotee of any god you like or fear. As a Jew, Paul, in contrast, insisted that there is only one true God, the sole Lord, though there are many rulers, most at war with one another. The rest of the gods, the mighty emperor included, are mere so-called gods, Paul implied. The consequence was the "secularization" of political authority and, ultimately, its democratization since the one God is necessarily the God of all.

Sophia didn't mention that in the letter to the church in Philippi, written some thirteen years after Paul's original visit, Paul composed or quoted an early Christian ode, which specifies the character of God's lordship and the Christian way of life and which is the key to Paul's political theology. If the scholars who argue that Paul borrowed it rather than composed it himself are right, this is one of the very earliest Christian statements of any kind we have. A *poem* about the person at the center of the Christian faith is the beginning of all Christian literature! Did Michael Edwards discuss that poem? Christ appears in it as a strange Lord, very unlike an emperor. Instead of holding graspingly to his divine status for fear of losing empire, he abandoned his heavenly throne and came into the world "stabling under a mean roof," as a twenty-one-year-old Milton put it, to serve humanity to the point of death. He revealed himself as the universal Lord through just such prodigious generosity. For his descent was, in a real sense, already his exaltation; in that act of love, he was as glorious as he ever was or would be. I find this Christ irresistibly moving. Writing this, I realized for the first time that a poem—its truth—is keeping me Christian.

The Freedom of a Christian is an interpretation of this poem (as are, in a very different way and with different emphases, Milton's *Paradise Lost* and *Paradise Regained*). In it, Luther sketched a compelling vision of the union of freedom and love rooted in the character of the very Source and Goal of everything that is. The free journey of the Son from the glory of equality with God to the ignominy of crucifixion is for Luther the key to both the nature of God and the dynamics of human freedom and service. God is not concerned with God's own glory and seeks no benefits from creatures. Being love and therefore loving without conditions, God instead confers benefits on creatures. That's the bedrock of Luther's vision. From this follow two seemingly contradictory claims about human life that structure the book:

> A Christian is a perfectly free lord of all, subject to none.
>
> A Christian is a perfectly dutiful servant of all, subject to all.

As Christ was before he took on the form of the servant, so Christians, united with Christ, are free "sovereigns" without having to do anything either to acquire or maintain their sovereignty; each is loved into their own particular form of being and continues to be loved for absolutely no reason at all. Because they don't need to establish themselves as "sovereigns," they are free to be dutiful servants of all without fear of loss. A bit like God, they can give to their neighbors in need without having to require anything in return.

As I have described it, the vision of Christian life Luther sketches is both highly religious (humans receive themselves in faith from God) and highly worldly (humans give themselves not to God directly but to neighbors in love), and in both ways very intimately "spiritual." And yet the ecclesiastical and political impacts of this vision of life were immense, in some ways revolutionary. Ask Hegel about it! It underpins much of Milton's ecclesiastical and political thought, Filippo Falcone, who wrote a PhD dissertation on liberty in Milton, tells me.

I discovered *The Freedom of a Christian* more than forty years ago as a doctoral student in Tübingen, Germany, in 1982, during the run-up to the five-hundred-year anniversary of Luther's birth, and I have loved it ever since. As my little present to Luther for his birthday, I translated the German version—Luther wrote it originally in Latin—into Croatian and wrote an introduction to it. Perhaps I exaggerated when I praised it to you on our walk and invoked Marilynne in support. I searched my inbox and found that she described it as "one of the most beautiful things in Christian literature. All literature." That's both less and more than what you reported that I said to you ("the supreme achievement of Western prose"). What she actually wrote seems just about right to me, even though I agree that most of her sentences—and yours, too—are crafted better than but a very few of the many that Luther wrote.

We keep returning to "religion." What does Michael Edwards mean by religion? If we were to unpack the layers of meaning in the phrase "This is my body" and the conditions of their possibility, I wonder what would be the proper word for that body of language and practice? Come to think of it, I don't know what exactly you mean by "religion." I am an avowed atheist when it comes to the God in which many people believe. Maybe I am similarly a-religious, even anti-religious. I will return to Bonhoeffer's account of religion-lessness in another letter. After rereading his *Letters and Papers from Prison*, I think I understand better what he was after. His position may or may not satisfy you, but it should help clarify things a bit around "religion."

"I have such a hunger for church—no, for *shared* prayer and praise—but have given up on having it fed." I don't know why this sentence surprised me. What do you find missing in the Book of Common Prayer? I am taken by it, especially the 1928 version. Whenever I am attentive and sometimes even when I am not, it returns me to myself by taking me to Christ.

Miroslav

PS. I am in Croatia, on the island of Ugljan, vacationing with Mira at my sister's place. Jessica was planning to be with us, but at the last moment she decided to travel instead to Bismarck. Her mother is not well, and we don't know how long she will be with us. I still see my father's eyes following me longingly when I left his hospital bed, after a strangely brief visit, never to see him alive again. I did come up with some thin excuse for my flight from fragility, and I have lived with regret since. I am so glad Jessica went.

When I am not in the clear waters of the Adriatic with Mira, and while she is playing with five of her cousins and three of their friends, I am reading. I brought with me Max Scheler's *Ressentiment* (1915), his response to Nietzsche's *On the Genealogy of Morality*. You may know the book, though I wouldn't be surprised if you don't. Scheler, a Jewish Protestant who converted to Catholicism, is largely forgotten, unjustly in my opinion. His thesis is that Nietzsche wrongly lumps the modern Western morality of his time with Christian morality in tracing both to *ressentiment*. Scheler claims that a genuinely Christian moral outlook is free from *ressentiment*. His key argument, no more than a few pages, concerns the nature of love, both human love for God and God's love for the world.

Very early in our correspondence, we touched on love for God—how God is always slipping somehow away from me as an intentional object, and how you are gripped by love for God. You returned briefly to the topic in your last letter, too. I don't think we clarified sufficiently what we mean by love, though. Perhaps Scheler can help. He draws a contrast, likely too sharply, between ancient Greek and Christian accounts of love. The most important difference, or rather, the most important indicator of the difference, is the *direction* of love's movement. "All ancient philosophers, poets, and moralists agree that love is striving, an aspiration of the 'lower' toward the 'higher.'" The beloved is always higher, the lover is always lower.

> The universe is a great chain . . . in which the lower always strives for and is attracted by the higher, which never turns back but aspires upward in its turn. This process continues up to the deity, which itself does not love, but represents the eternally unmoving and unifying *goal* of all these aspirations of love.

In this account, love is a vehicle that carries one to the state of nonlove. In the Christian account, the direction of movement is reversed.

> An event that is monstrous for the man of antiquity, that is absolutely paradoxical according to its axioms, is

> supposed to have taken place in Galilee: God spontaneously "descended" to man, became servant, and died the bad servant's death on the cross! Now the precept of loving good and hating evil, loving one's friend and hating one's enemy, becomes meaningless. There is no longer any "highest good" independent of and beyond the act and movement of love! Love itself is the highest of all goods! The *summum bonum* is no longer a value of a thing, but of an act, the value of love itself *as love*—not for its results and achievements.

All God's acts have the character of this act of love, God's creating and preserving and not just redeeming. Whence this reversal? asks Scheler. It is unlikely that *ressentiment* is its source.

For the foundation of the argument, Scheler turns to that Christian poem from Philippians 2 that was central to Luther. There he finds that the "great urge to love, to serve, to bend down, is God's own essence." And there he also finds that just such a God is to be the object of human love and emulation. I cannot claim that I emulate the Lord who became servant. I fled the fragility of my own father! But I find this God irresistibly attractive. John the Evangelist draws a similar sketch of God and love by telling a story about Jesus's meal on the evening before his crucifixion. Knowing that "all things" were in his hands, writes John, knowing also "that he had come from God and was going to God," Jesus got up from his last meal, took off his outer robe, tied a towel around his waist, poured water into a basin, washed his disciples' feet, and wiped them with the towel. His last act was a service so demeaning that a Jewish master was not permitted to force even a Jewish slave to do it.

That's how I "justify" to myself loving *Love*, which is God's being and God's act. And loving Love makes it possible for me to live with the inability to make God an intentional "object" of my longing.

AUGUST 27

Dear Miroslav,

It's good to be back in touch. I have been in England, Tennessee, Texas, and Maine. Far too much travel. By the end, even the lake in Maine we stayed just steps from, so still and serene it seemed a rival sky, frazzled me.

We were in Texas to see my family. As you know, my mother, brother, sister, and her eldest son all live in a small apartment near Fort Worth. Their various afflictions are too much to go into. My sister's other son, Michael, lives with his wife and infant daughter down the road. Michael and his wife are strict Church of Christ people and while we were there persuaded us (Danielle, me, and our daughters) to spend a morning working in a food bank at the church. The poverty was shocking, a seemingly endless line of cars with all manner of misery spilling out of them. Equally shocking was how *hard* everyone was working to package the food, load the carts, and deliver them to the waiting families. By the end we were all drenched in sweat (it was 106 degrees), our egos incinerated, determined to make this part of our lives when we returned to New Haven. It was the best thing we did in all our travels.

What is religion? That church subscribes to dogmas you and I would both find appalling. The God they serve is the one who makes you an "atheist." And yet look at the love—for what else could you call it?—that led those parishioners to spend day after day (the food bank is open seven days a week) ensuring that hungry people could eat. I didn't hear a word about God. The recipients were not evangelized in any way, not even with a piece of paper that invited them to church or put the charity in any Christian context. They simply drove away with their trunks filled with food.

For years I assumed that what Bonhoeffer meant by his "religion-less Christianity" was just what anyone would expect: Christ without Christianity, freedom from the whole institutional edifice—churches, creeds, doctrines, all the internecine battles that have turned Christianity into a million little religions, each convinced of its own purity and rightness. This is shocking because, as you know, Bonhoeffer was a pretty orthodox Lutheran pastor and wrote books like *Life Together* and *The Cost of Discipleship*. But since we were last in touch I've read *Bonhoeffer's Religionless Christianity in Its Christological Context* by Peter Hooten and realize that I've always been mistaken. What Bonhoeffer wanted "freedom" from (and, of course,

Luther was in his bones) was the metaphysical pressure that faith has acquired. He never said so, but I think it might even be somewhat congruent with my own notion that the great poison of Protestantism is its notion of faith, this enormous pressure that is put on some internal assent.

I find this all quite confusing and have no answers. It's no good saying that the actions of those Church of Christ members show that dogma is simply irrelevant and what matters is what one *does*. I think their beliefs have palpable negative consequences, particularly on the lives of women. (But then most of those volunteers *were* women and presumably would disagree with me.) I also find it dissatisfying to say that I am an "atheist" when it comes to the God they believe in, since their God seems to lead them toward expressions of charity that I certainly can't manage in my own life. I can't seem to abide "religion" (in the obvious sense), find myself crawling out of my skin in church. Yet I do crave communal worship, and without religion that food bank would not exist and hundreds of people would be going hungry. As I say, I have no answers. What I do know is that I'm through *thinking* about all of this and resolve to put more of my life in service to others, whatever form that takes.

As for the Book of Common Prayer, sure, I find it very beautiful. But Episcopalianism is *chilly*, and wealthy, and white. Its doctrines require no intellectual contortions or dishonesty, and you know how much I admire Rowan Williams. The Australian bishop John V. Taylor has also taught me an enormous amount. Yet every time I go to an Episcopal church, there I am again, bored, anxious, trying to reconcile this cosmic lassitude with the fire I feel in my heart. I usually slip out before the service is over. I'm willing to admit that the problem is me.

So as always I return to, take my refuge in, art. Fosse's *Septology* is in some ways an odd book for me to love. The prose is flat, for one thing, which I usually can't abide. I also have an aversion to books that have no breathing space, and his single sentence over seven volumes can feel quite constrictive, even maddening. I came to see both of these aspects of the book as essential to its effort to create, and immerse the reader within, the consciousness of this artist, Asle, whose gift is images, not words (a suddenly lovely sentence, a bit of "style," would break the spell), and who is in fact having a kind of breakdown in the book (thus the sense of constriction).

Two things especially moved me. Each book begins with an image—the "St. Anthony's cross" he has just painted—and ends with a series of Latin prayers: Art prepares for, enables, and eventually gives way to faith. Art is a *means*, not an end. I doubt I need to explain why this movement is so piercing to me.

The second thing is the nature of Asle's faith. It is expressed in his art, for one thing—that dark radiance that you mention and that he tries to describe over and over in the book, the one light that all the paintings at once contain and fall short of. That faith is also expressed in his Catholicism. You feel some idiosyncrasy in his devotion, and he is solitary in his faith in a way that would seem counter to Christian teaching—even at Mass you feel how *alone* he is. But he does go to Mass, and Catholicism provides the structure of his faith. (Catholicism seems to accommodate idiosyncratic expressions of faith, even outright diversions of doctrine, better than Protestantism, which is forever splitting in new sects. At the parish Danielle attends, the priest makes clear that communion is open to *everyone*, thus ignoring this especially odious point of Catholic doctrine—odious because I can't imagine Jesus turning *anyone* away from Communion.)

Most of all, though, what I love is the way Asle expresses his faith (aside from the art, I mean). At one point he is speaking about what he believes and he stops himself to say, no, that's not right, it's not that I believe, it's more that I *know* God is real. That's it. When I think of what drives me in search of God, it is the same inner imperative by which I know I love Danielle, the same energy I follow when a poem is just occurring to me. I have lived my life, which has been difficult but has been *mine*, by instinct, and all of my instincts tell me I must follow God. I simply *know* that he is.

I should also say that I love the sheer quietude of the book, the way it almost seems preverbal, as if you really were "hearing" someone's thoughts.

Michael Edwards does bring up that hymn from Philippians, but what you say about it is more interesting than what he does. Here's the hymn:

> Who, being in very nature God,
>   did not consider equality with God something to be used to his own advantage;
> rather, he made himself nothing
>   by taking the very nature of a servant,
>   being made in human likeness.
> And being found in appearance as a man,
>   he humbled himself
>   by becoming obedient to death—
>   even death on a cross!

"Obedient to death" is the startling phrase for me. In Miltonic terms, to be obedient to Death is to be obedient to Satan, who is Death's father (if I am remembering correctly). God had to consent to what was anathema to him—not to overcome it, which he could have done through power, but in order to preserve human freedom, and in order to truly commune with us. Just imagine how beautiful religion could be if the true Christ were at its heart.

The first two lines of the hymn (even clunkily translated as they are) pack quite a theological wallop as well. Essentially, God's nature is to ignore his nature; God's nature is to be not-God. At the end of my last book I focus on a passage from Isaiah: "Is there a God beside me?" Yahweh asks, before providing his own answer, "Yea, there is no God." I realize what is meant here—the answer is obviously "no"—but it's a striking way to put it. It's hard not to hear a hyphen implied, no-God as God's twin. I think this is what Vattimo is trying to get at: The apparent erasure of God from Western culture is the fruition of this moment in scripture. I don't "agree" with this—I can't find anything redemptive in the nihilism I see around me—but I do admire the effort to read the scripture into the current moment, to not give up, to somehow sacralize this particular despair.

This is getting long, but I have more to say! I find your paragraphs on loving God very lucid and convincing. You might remember that on one of our walks I brought up a passage from Ortega y Gasset who said that we can only fall in love with some form of superiority. We recognize some quality in ourselves in greater abundance, or more likely in finer form, in someone else. "Superiority" has the wrong connotation, as there is nothing competitive or even hierarchical in the recognition; we are lifted up by it, ennobled. I have been very fortunate in my life to have experienced such love in my marriage. I feel that my conversations with you are helping me to understand what such love looks like with regard to God.

And like you, I find the picture of God/Jesus that comes through in that passage from Philippians very attractive and convincing. Often I think I am a deist obsessed with Jesus. God we can't know aside from certain mystical experiences, which can be transformative but are fugitive, elusive, and in an ineluctable sense impersonal. (I am baffled when people talk about their "relationship" with God.) People's experiences of God are so different. On the cross Jesus says, "*My* God, my God, why have you forsaken me?" which I take to be a deep theological insight. There is no collective God; his nature is to have a particular reality and being for everyone who seeks him (and perhaps, too, for those who don't). This is why I put such emphasis on the quality of the attention we bring to him. But God has given us Jesus, has become Jesus, so that we might know him more intimately and immediately, in the peaks and pains of ordinary existence, in "mere" matter.

The temptation is to reduce Jesus to entirely human dimensions. That Jesus suffered as we suffer is a consolation, as well as warrant to his truth: We wouldn't take him seriously otherwise. That his desolation and sense of abandonment speak right into our modern nihilism attests to that perdurable truth. Thus Vattimo or (again) Rilke:

> He went up under the gray leaves
> all gray and dissolved in olive country
> and laid his forehead full of dust
> deep in the dustiness of burning hands.
>
> To end like this. And this *was* the end.
> Now I am to go, while I go blind,
> and why is it Your will that I must say
> You are, when I myself no longer find You.

I no longer find You. Not in me.
Not in those others. Not in this rock.
I no longer find you. I am alone.

I am alone with all of human grief,
which through You I understood to lighten,
You who are not. O shame unnameable.

—Translated by
Edward Snow

That really gets at something. Jesus doesn't find God inside himself, nor in others, nor in nature ("Not in this rock"). His destitution is absolute and is *shameful*. That last line could be read different ways: Is God the shame, or is it the action of having sacrificed his life for nothing? I have felt this level of bereft. But that passage in Philippians speaks of Jesus's entire life and nature; the cross is simply the culminating instance. And actually the hymn continues (it seems a continuation, at least):

Therefore God exalted him to the highest place
  and gave him the name that is above every name,

that at the name of Jesus every knee should bow,
  in heaven and on earth and under the earth,
and every tongue acknowledge that Jesus Christ is Lord,
  to the glory of God the Father.

I wish the scripture didn't split God and Jesus here, that it more credibly fused the two. (One can read the last two lines that way, but one has to have that interpretation in hand; the verse doesn't naturally suggest that.) But the point is that Jesus's divinity overcomes his humanity. No. The fruition of his humanity is divinity; humanity overcomes itself. I recently read the philosopher Jacob Needleman's book *What Is God?*, in which he has this provocative formulation: "Modernity: the realization of freedom *from*. The necessary new era: the call of what freedom is *for*." Needleman thinks the answer is brand new. I have thought that myself at times but am wavering. Luther's formulation, as you have it, seems appealing: Freedom is both spiritual autonomy with regard to God and humble servitude with regard to humanity. It's appallingly simple—but so very difficult to live out. Maybe you'll turn me into a Lutheran after all.

Chris

SEPTEMBER 6

Dear Chris,

Three quick comments about God, and then I will turn to Jesus, to start a more focused conversation about your "obsession" with him—and mine, too. Among other things, I would like to understand the experience you described in your Easter Sunday letter: Christ coming to you and *becoming* you when you were near death and suffered terribly.

It was a bit tongue-in-cheek that I described myself as an "atheist" with respect to my colleague's crude image of God. "Atheists" is what some polytheist neighbors of the early Christians called them because they contested the divinity of their gods. Christians are like Diagoras of Melos, an atheist, who "chopped up the wooden statue of Hercules to boil his turnips." (The quote is from Athenagoras, a second-century philosopher and Christian, who is, I think, the first to mention that early Christians were accused of atheism—along with cannibalism and incest.) I was riffing on that accusation. I share much of your sensibility about the relation between practices and belief in God. It is possible to affirm a false god with one's beliefs while obeying the true God with one's practices. And the other way around, too. Beliefs embedded in right practices—right orientation of the "heart," to echo both the prophet Isaiah and Jesus who quotes him—are more important than some free-floating "assent" to "truths" about God.

Here, as earlier in our correspondence, you push strongly against the idea of a "collective God." I agree with your concern expressed in this denial. As any good parent's relation to a child is tailored to the character of the child, God's relation to a person is tailored to the character of that person. And yet, a good parent is a parent to all their children together, attending not just to each but to their relation to one another and to the common space they inhabit. God is the God of each person and of the whole world in all relations that constitute it. The "one" correlates with both "each" and "the whole." If God were not the God of all, God would dissipate for us all into "divine individuals" and each of them drawn into our fraught relations with one another. In *The Antichrist*, Nietzsche argues that a national God—meaning a god of a particular nation—is always will to power. This transmutation of God to will to power is in the logic of God being the God of a particular nation or a particular person without at the same time being the God of the whole world.

The way you read the phrase that Jesus Christ was "obedient to death" in Philippians 2 would be wonderful poetry and fascinating theology. Alas, "to" is an ambiguous translation of Greek *mechri*, which means "until, to the point of." Christ's obedience is to God, not to Death. I read the hymn to say that, before the journey into servanthood, Christ was, in some (at the time) not-yet-specified sense, equal to God. After that journey, he was given "the name that is above every name," which can only be the unpronounceable name of the God of Israel (the point which is reflected also in his designation as *kyrios* or "Lord," which the ancient Greek translators of the Hebrew Bible used to render YHWH). The one who is equal with God becomes servant to the point of death, and, on account of this deed, is then publicly and universally recognized as God. Though I hesitate to see here the fruition of humanity into divinity as you do, we agree about the point of the passage: Jesus's journey discloses the very essence of divinity—and portrays it at the same time as the way of life. An injunction introduces the hymn: "Let the same mind be in you that was in Christ Jesus."

"Just imagine how beautiful religion could be if the true Christ were at its heart," you write. I imagined. And I sighed. As I must have mentioned on one of our walks, I have come to think that Jesus Christ has become a moral stranger in today's cultures of late modernity. He is a stranger to those who call themselves by his name and not just to those who have barely heard of him, who have no interest in rectifying that lack or any sense there is anything there to rectify at all. Most of what is important to us—looks, money, sex, social esteem, success—does not seem to have been important to him. We have no idea how he looked; he had no possessions of his own; he never had intercourse; when word of him spread in a region, he would withdraw into solitude or go elsewhere; in obedience to God, he seems to have intentionally headed straight into what all those around him thought was a colossal failure. Most of what was important to him—purity of desire, going a second mile, forgiving innumerable times, serving the lowly, for instance—is odious to us. It's not that there isn't any overlap between our values and his—the sick ought to be healed, the hungry fed, the sorrowing comforted—but we mostly want to get paid in some form for such activities rather than doing them freely. Jesus, an irrelevant moral stranger.

A few years back, I taught a course with Drew Collins called Jesus and Being Human. It was about how our lives might look if we took the life of Jesus Christ to be paradigmatic. During one seminar session, we discussed the passage from the Gospels where Jesus rebukes his disciples for not letting parents bring their children for him to bless them. "Let the little children come to me, and do not stop them," he tells the disciples, "for it is to such as these that the kingdom of heaven belongs." A touching scene, especially in the ancient world not known for its tenderness toward children. Mira, my daughter, was one year old at the time, and Drew, too, had small children. One of us wondered aloud whether we could imagine letting Jesus raise our kids. We both balked at the idea, viscerally, as if some unspecified but great damage would befall them if committed to his care. He can bless them, but we will not let him take charge of raising them. What were we thinking? That he would not know what their best interests were? That he would not keep their best interests in view? What did we imply that Jesus was good for? With his touch to keep harm, as we defined it, at bay and fortune close? To save in some eternal sense, get people into the "kingdom" after they die? To assist in holding together the darkness and light that are our ordinary lives? To remind us that grace encompasses all humanity, and that all children are above average? In every one of these ways of being for us, he would be some kind of beneficent help on the way. But he would not be the way, not the model of life we actually ought to live. He would be a loving force, for me, though not in any deeper sense than being at my disposal to sustain me and make me thrive. I myself, and in the way I define the good of my life, would then be the terminal point of his love for me. This is not entirely wrong, but it cannot be more than only partly right.

He did make those in need terminal points of his love: He fed the hungry, healed the sick, raised the dead. (I don't think I ever asked you how you think of the role of Christ in your Lazarus-come-out-of-the-tomb experience this past Easter, given the technological wonder of modern medicine involved?) But Jesus summed up much of what he was after in what feels like a very uncomfortable, almost cruel, injunction: "Whoever does not take up the cross and follow me is not worthy of me." The cross here is not some unspecified suffering that befalls us, but service to others and the pain that may result from it. Denying oneself is not self-diminishment, but again service to others without regard for one's comfort or status. If I am not filling the trunks of the hungry in 106°F humid Texas heat—which I have never done—I am not worthy of Christ and cannot be his disciple! And as I am filling the trunks of the hungry with food, if I am loving myself and my superior magnanimity rather than loving the people I am serving and regarding them as more valuable than I am myself, I am worthy neither of Christ nor of my own true self! The self that actively loves his neighbor is the terminal point of God's love for me. Somewhere deep down, I do desire to take Mira's hand and together with her follow the radical, uncomfortable Christ. I suspect that many people do. But that desire is buried too deep down, covered with the mud of ordinary living and the boulders of the inertias of modernity in which we think we must participate or perish. It is sometimes hard even to recognize it as a genuine moral desire on which we ought to act. It feels more like lunacy. I know that it isn't, perhaps in the kind of way you know that God is real.

"Who is Christ actually for us today?" asked Bonhoeffer not long before he was murdered in prison. His "today" was Hitler's madness and the modern world that had lost its erstwhile religious longing and acquired a sense of autonomy, of its ability to manage life without "religion." But the figure of Jesus was still attractive. As Bonhoeffer puts it in *Letters and Papers from Prison*, as "the human being for others," Jesus is our "experience of transcendence." Our "today" is much like Bonhoeffer's, except that Christ has become to us a stranger. Surprisingly, perhaps, God seems to us closer than Christ. The "tables of value," to use

Nietzsche's term, with which we operate place not so much an epistemological limit but an "ethico-social limit" to our ability to imagine that Jesus Christ makes a genuine "claim" on us as citizens of "the world that has come of age." How can we recover existential *resonance* with Christ?

In Fosse's *Septology*, each of its seven books culminates with its protagonist, Asle, making the turn from art to religion. The tangible symbol of the turn is Asle taking the rosary off of his neck and placing his thumb and index finger on its brown wooden cross to begin praying the "Our Father," "The Jesus Prayer," and "Ave Maria." He is not sure whether God exists or not. If God exists, Asle does not know what the relation between God and him is—whether God comes first and then he as God's creature, whether he comes first and God comes into existence through him, or whether the two happen somehow simultaneously, as he had read in Meister Eckhart. But the wood of the cross is smooth, and, troubled man that he is, he needs consolation. "Come to me, all you that are weary and are carrying heavy burdens, and I will give you rest," I imagine the cross telling his heart through his thumb and index finger.

Most of the time, I carry a pocket cross with me. When I was returning from Croatia in the middle of August, I was at the airport in Zagreb settled with Mira in the waiting room past the security check. I reached into my right-hand pocket. The cross was missing. I was mortified and frantically searched everywhere, and then remembered that I had taken it out and placed it into the bin at the security check. I rushed back and in anguish asked the agents whether they had found a small iron cross. Even before I finished, I could see one of them reaching to get it. Croatia is a very Catholic country, and when he handed me the lost treasure, he said, "Don't you lose *this*!" I did not need the lesson, but appreciated it nonetheless. "Where did you get it?" he then asked. "A friend, an artist, made it for me," I said, after thanking him profusely. Some twenty-five years ago, Rich Polson, an amateur artist from Vancouver, read my book *Exclusion and Embrace* and, moved by it, made a metal sculpture of the Crucified, which now sits on my desk. When you look at it from above, the stylized arms of Christ spread out and with his head bent down he looks like a dove in gentle flight, but long nails hold it fastened to a rusted and rugged cross. Twenty years later, Rich gave me a little iron pocket cross. Its front is textured, pounded with the narrow side of the hammer, but smooth, inviting touch. When I feel like Asle, I hold the cross and my thumb runs gently up and down and to the sides over the front.

The back is flat, with sharp edges and pointy corners. Even when I touch the front, my hand feels the uncomfortable back. That is Jesus Christ to me. Consolation, but also challenge, cutting and painful. Both are, I feel, sculpting me into myself.

Who is Christ for you?

Miroslav

PS. What an extraordinary poem by Rilke. Christ consoles because his experiences with God are so close to our anguish. But he strikes with terror. The shame—whichever of the two ways of reading it you note we opt for—comes not because some misfortune has befallen him notwithstanding his faithfulness to God (which is Job's ordeal) but because he suffers and is abandoned *as a result* of his faithfulness to God. To me, that is one of the most uncomfortable things about Christ. Maybe that's why I hesitate when I imagine the possibility of Jesus raising my daughter.

OCTOBER 10

Dear Miroslav,

I was going to do a Deriddean defense of my inspired misprision ("obedient to death"), but I can't (thankfully) remember a word of Derrida. Ignorance is rising in me like the warming seas.

Before I turn to Jesus, I want to reach back to what you said in the letter before last about your understanding of loving God as loving love. I follow what you're saying, and like you I find the character of Jesus that comes through in those details very compelling—though I also immediately thought of the end of Stevie Smith's poem "Was He Married?" in which two very modern voices are discussing Jesus:

> A god is Man's doll, you ass,
> He makes him up like this on purpose.
>
> He might have made him up worse.
>
> He often has, in the past.

To choose a god of love, as he did and does,
Is a little move then?

Yes, it is.

A larger one will be when men
Love love and hate hate but do not deify
them?

It will be a larger one.

The irony here is that Jesus might agree. If we could simply "love love" without deifying that action, if love were coextensive with being, then we would be living in God so completely that we wouldn't need the name.

But I have to say, I don't really know what this would mean aside from actions in the world, which indeed is what you reach for with the foot-washing story. I think we're caught in a tautology. If we understand God as love, the problem of how to love God is not clarified by simply swapping the terms. We're not released from the objectlessness of God. And though Jesus *does* refer to actions in the world when he tells Peter to "feed my sheep," it seems clear that he means something besides that when he says (via Deuteronomy) that we must love God with our whole hearts, minds, and souls.

Perhaps we are meant to love reality? I'm sure I've quoted this poem to you before:

A Prayer That Will Be Answered

Lord let me suffer much and then die
Let me walk through silence
and leave nothing behind not even fear
Make the world continue
let the ocean kiss the sand just as before
Let the grass stay green
so that the frogs can hide in it
so that someone can bury his face in it
and sob out his love
Make the day rise brightly
as if there were no more pain

And let my poem stand clear as a windowpane
bumped by a bumblebee's head

—Anna Kamieńska,
translated by Stanisław
Barańczak and Clare
Cavanagh

I love this because it seems to me a beautiful expression of what it might mean to love reality *as it is*, which includes suffering, pain, and death but also a poem clear as a windowpane against which the bee of a reader's mind can bump, the little ripple of mystery that goes through brute reality *when we have loved it for itself alone*.

But it's not easy to love reality. I'm certain I have never managed it (and I doubt Nietzsche, for all his notion of tragic joy, did). Why would the chief injunction of our lives be so nearly impossible?

I doubt it would. I expect you know exactly what it means to love God. And I expect I do, too. And I expect it doesn't mean the same thing to either of us, and that neither of us is ultimately able to put it into words. But we *know* it. That's the entire reason I pray, because I love God and want to be with him. Yes, the love I have for Danielle leads to love of God; and yes, the love that moves through me when I am able to write a real poem seems to me both of God and for God; and yes, when I act in life with (so far as I can discern) genuine charity I feel that I am participating in the love of God. But still, there is something else. There is me without anyone else in the world, and without poetry, and certainly without religion, and it is that "me" that is being called to love God. I bow my head and I do it. I can't explain it any further than that.

Though there is this:

A True Hymne

MY joy, my life, my crown!
My heart was meaning all the day,
Somewhat it fain would say:
And still it runneth mutt'ring up and down
With onely this, *My joy, my life, my crown.*

Yet slight not these few words:
If truly said, they may take part
Among the best in art.

The finenesse which a hymne or psalme affords,
Is, when the soul unto the lines accords.

He who craves all the minde,
And all the soul, and strength, and time,
If the words onely ryme,
Justly complains, that somewhat is behinde
To make his verse, or write a hymne in kinde.

Whereas if th' heart be moved,
Although the verse be somewhat scant,
God doth supplie the want.
As when th' heart sayes (sighing to be approved)
O, could I love! And stops: God writeth, *Loved.*

George Herbert suggests here that if we do as I have suggested, if we try to love God in whatever form we understand that to be (poetry, in this instance), if we bring our whole hearts even though we feel the frailness and inadequacy of our abilities, then God will complete and perfect the action. And that completion consists in his love for us, which, after all, is the source of any love we are able to have for him—any love we have for *anything.*

Now, Jesus. As I have suggested in other letters, I really do take seriously the notion that God and Jesus are one. When God entered the world, he entered it wholly. When Jesus died on the cross, God died. (Jesus as God's "son" I can only read as metaphor, a vestige of pre-Christian religions. Of course, it's *all* metaphor insofar as we don't have the capacity to fully understand this relation.)

I have mentioned the time when I felt so close to Jesus, the months of my first bone marrow transplant in Chicago. I say "Jesus" and not "God" because the relation felt so fleshed and material—interactions with loved ones and strangers, the natural world (by which I mean also the city, the metal machine of central Chicago). I wasn't accompanied, I was inhabited, and the world burned with something too intrinsic to interpret or question. It didn't *mean*. It shone with a radiance that precedes—and precludes—meaning.

And I say "Jesus" and not "God" because I think the experience had everything to do with the crucifixion. I have written a lot about this and don't want to repeat myself. I am not one to valorize or automatically ennoble suffering. I have had my share of it, have witnessed my loved ones crushed and degraded by it, have myself been crushed and degraded by it. But I know, too, that there can be a mysterious light in suffering, a clarity that suffering doesn't merely enable but actually is. And this is so because God, in taking human suffering upon himself, sacralized it for those who can see with his eyes—*Christ's* eyes—in those moments.

Tomáš Halík suggests that we tend to think of the crucifixion and the resurrection as two acts of a drama, the latter triumphing over the former. This is a mistake, he says. We should think of it as a single act. The resurrection *reinterprets* the crucifixion, rather than serving as merely a "happy ending." If we can link that story to the story of our own life, if we can see our suffering in light of Jesus's, then we can live in hope. We are not freed from the reality of pain and death—the promise of an afterlife, for me, is cold comfort, as it's a function of the imagination, and the imagination is powerless in the face of extreme suffering. But we can be freed to suffer in a way that is not meaningless and strengthened to reconcile it with our lives. I taught James Baldwin's "Sonny's Blues" this week, and late in that masterpiece Sonny says, in response to his brother's statement that there's no way not to suffer: "No, there's no way not to suffer. But you try all kinds of ways to keep from drowning in it, to keep on top of it, and to make it seem—well, like *you*." "Whát I dó is me, for that I came," says Hopkins in a famous sonnet. But this follows:

> I say móre: the just man justices;
> Keeps grace: thát keeps all his goings graces;
> Acts in God's eye what in God's eye he is—
> Chríst—for Christ plays in ten thousand places,
> Lovely in limbs, and lovely in eyes not his
> To the Father through the features of men's faces.

Who is Jesus for me? He is the one who makes suffering sacred, the one who harmonizes love and action, the one who makes it possible to love God.

Chris

OCTOBER 24

Dear Chris,

Why did I pedantically push against your arresting interpretation of Christ's "obedience to death" in *Carmen Christi* by quibbling about the meaning of an original Greek preposition? I would not have demurred had I been reading the poem simply as literature. But I am not. I am reading it as literature that is also a *sacred text.* Sacred texts are polysemous, too. "If you read a text twice and it means the same thing, you haven't read it rightly." This, or something close to it, is Ibn Arabi, a Sufi, speaking of reading the Qur'an. The same, I think, is true of reading the Bible, especially if you take it that God speaks through it. If God is alive and if every human is in time, the meanings of sacred texts will shift and change, even if ever so slightly. It isn't possible to step twice into the same sacred river; every reading of the sacred text is different because we change. Still, when it comes to sacred texts, the play of meanings presupposes the stability of the text itself. I want translators, and interpreters who follow them, to honor the vocabulary and grammar in the original—to the extent that is possible with ancient texts.

For me, this is a happy constraint, bustling with its own kind of liveliness. I suspect that you might chafe under it.

I first noticed this difference in our readings of biblical texts when we discussed the book of Job in our class on suffering. You were happy to lop off the introductory and concluding narratives from the text—sections that most scholars think are later editorial additions—and read the large body of its extraordinary poetry on its own terms. You could then plausibly suggest, as you did also recently in that wonderful review of Michael Edwards's *The Bible and Poetry* in *Commonweal*, that in Job's very first speech, so impious to his sanctimonious comforters, he in fact curses God in cursing the day on which he was born. God would then have lost the bet that the lopped-off introduction tells us God made with Satan. Reading Job as a sacred text, I, in contrast, take the introductory and concluding sections to belong integrally to the body of the book as its narrative frame. Since God at the end says that Job spoke rightly of God, God must have won the bet. In the first speech, Job did not actually curse God, though in cursing God's creation he came a hair's breadth away from doing so. The drama of the remainder of the book rests on the uncertainty over whether Job's anguish, having brought him to the very edge of the cliff, will, with the help of his comforters' condescension, push him over it. I don't think my interpretation is better than yours. It's different, a function of my reading Job as a sacred text. There is something really beautiful and true about your reading: God's love isn't rattled by Job's curse.

If *deification* is involved in the claim that God is love, Stevie Smith is right: A smaller move would be to project love onto God and the larger one would be to call love itself divine. This was exactly Ludwig Feuerbach's point in *The Essence of Christianity* (1841): Human beings debase themselves when they worship their own essence externalized onto God. (The English translation, by George Eliot, is a wonderful read—for a philosophical text.) I am tempted by the projection theory of religion, and often succumb to it, not at the level of a general theory of religion, but in daily religious practice. Despite all the little projections of mine that I detect in my image of God, I have made a wager of trust that God was not invented so that we could have a screen onto which to project the beauty of love or justify the ugliness of hatred. Instead, God has poured the Love that God is into the material object that was the body of Jesus Christ so that we humans could see, hear, smell, touch, and taste love's incarnation. In Jesus, the God who is Love steps out of the objectlessness of transcendence and becomes an itinerant "object" in the world. This is why I prefer to write not of "loving love" but of "loving Love," short for "loving the One who is Love." The only way I know how to love God is by loving the kind of love Jesus embodies. (I think that I should write here that I love Jesus, but that seems too sentimental for how I in fact relate to him.) And loving Love just *is* loving what Love loves. Augustine puts it beautifully: "For when we love charity, we love her loving something, precisely because she does love something."

Building on George Herbert's "O, could I love!," you write of trying to "love God in whatever form we understand that to be," of bringing our whole hearts into loving—and of God attending to our love's flaws and perfecting it. When I read such an account of Christian life, I realize how Protestant I am, in the classical sense of that term. There is a technical term in medieval theology for what Herbert and you describe: *facere quot in se est*—to do what is in one. I find the idea indeterminate and unachievable. When have I ever done all that I could, for God then to complete my work? I am mostly half-hearted, slothful to do the good. My love needs God at the beginning of my efforts and in the middle of them, too, rather than showing up after I have proven myself worthy on my own. I need the comfort of God's love *not* to be predicated on my achievement.

The poem assumes that the questions "What does it mean to love?" and "What are the proper objects of love?" are settled; only "the verse be somewhat scant," Herbert writes, not quite what it would need to be. I find answers to these questions, too, not settled in my actual practice of loving. I sometimes love in good conscience what I should not, and when I do love what I should, I often don't love it *as* I should. I should be able to do better. Christian "tables of values," to use Nietzsche's phrase, are simple: The two greatest commandments are to love God and love neighbor. I embrace them as my "hypergoods," to use Charles Taylor's term, the goods "which not only are incomparably more important than others but provide the standpoint from which these must be weighed, judged, decided about." But there are many kinds of love, which makes wholeheartedness in loving, though important, insufficient. With characteristically vivid bluntness, Luther wrote of our tendency to "love God as lice love a tramp; far from being interested in his welfare, their one concern is to feed on him and suck his blood." "Lice love" is no love and may be worse than the absence of love. He insisted on loving God for God's sake.

But should I love God for God's sake alone? Should I love neighbors for themselves alone? You push against "lice love," whether its object is God or any entity in the world. With Anna Kamieńska—what a poem!—you embrace love for reality "as it is" and, with surprising radicality, also "for itself alone." The gain from such a self-forgetful act is the immense treasure of "the little ripple of mystery that goes through brute reality," as you put it so beautifully. I admire—but am not sure. I don't think I was ever able to love anything for itself *alone*. But that is neither here nor there when it comes to what I *should* have done. What I aspire is to love God and neighbor for themselves, *too*—in God's case, *primarily*—but without bracketing myself as I love them.

I can think of three distinct variants of love for reality, none of them compatible with both of the others. You mentioned Nietzsche and the relation to the world he called *amor fati*. This is love for the entirety of what was and is, with every single one of its most horrid things, a desire for all of it to recur everlastingly. To love the world, which after God's death became "de-deified, stupid, blind, insane and questionable," we must give up the illusion of the "happiness" of the poor atheist "bird that felt itself free" from the Master of the Universe; it still keeps slamming against the walls of the cage that for Nietzsche is, paradoxically, the infinity of the cosmos itself.

Spinoza's *amor dei* stands in sharp contrast to Nietzsche's *amor fati*. For the pantheist Spinoza, the entirety of reality is God. Love for reality is a harmonious agreement with the universe as an expression of divine reason. Love is therefore an act of intellect that assents to reality, whereas, for Nietzsche, it is an act of will by which distance and rupture are bridged in "a powerful act of defiant affirmation," as Yirmiyahu Yovel has put it in his comparison of Spinoza's *amor dei* and Nietzsche's *amor fati*.

Distinct from both is love for the world in John's Gospel—and the Bible more broadly. "For God so loved the world that he gave his only Son" so that none would perish but all have everlasting life. This presumes that one can love the entire world without loving everything in it, as one can love one's child without loving everything a child does or everything a child has become. A loving Yes to reality requires, even consists in, a robust No to some of its features—including No to all those who hate under the guise of love, or practice mere "lice love." If Christ of the *Carmen Christi* was "obedient to death," then it was to overcome death through such obedience, take its sting away, which is what you might have had in mind when you disregarded the ordinary meaning of the Greek preposition.

Three very different ways of construing reality and loving it: Reality construed as divine and loved with intellectual assent; reality construed as chaotic and loved as an act of defying, Yes-saying will; reality construed as creation in the grip of evil and loved in imitation of Christ's practice of liberation. You suggest that I (Miroslav) "know exactly what it means to love." "Know" is a very strong word and "exactly" makes it into an impossibility. Whatever I tentatively and always provisionally know about what it means to love I know because I have embraced Jesus Christ as the incarnation of God's love for the world. His story and his teaching define love for me.

What do you make of Christ's teaching in the Gospels? You have not mentioned it in answering who Christ is for you.

Miroslav

PS. In my responses to your letters, I find myself often leaving on the table, without a comment, some amazing gems. In your last letter you wrote about the closeness of Jesus to you in extreme suffering. "I wasn't accompanied, I was inhabited, and the world burned with something too intrinsic to interpret or question. It didn't *mean*. It shone with a radiance that precedes—and precludes—meaning." This being inhabited by God in extreme suffering and experiencing radiance not so much of God but of the *material world* seems so unexpected, but I find it intuitively plausible and deeply right. It resonates with reports of the impact of conversion on one's experience of the world in James's *The Varieties of Religious Experience*, which I mentioned earlier. Astonishing that the unity of suffering and Jesus's presence made even the urban "metal machine" burn with transcendent fire! I don't know whether I told you my crazy idea, now in print in *The Home of God*, that in the book of Revelation the entire New Jerusalem, symbolically perched on Mt. Sinai with its tall walls made out of translucent red jasper, is portrayed as the burning bush of God's presence in Exodus 3.

NOVEMBER 27

Dear Miroslav,

Is death one of the parts of reality that you would say "no" to? I often feel this about Christianity as a whole, that it has set its face against death, has declared it unnatural to our souls. (Think of Milton.) It's why so much of Christianity has, for me, either an air of evasion, or a braced, determined, and tattered aspect to it, set as it is against the central fact of existence. My own soul inclines toward Kamieńska's vision, which is life in line with death rather than opposed to it, like a cypress on some high cliffside that grows fluent in torment, its limbs so adapted to disaster that it not only takes its shape from that which would—and one day will—end it, but thrives in the blast.

What makes a book "sacred"? And how do you decide what to keep and what to discard? If we learn that some passage has been tinkered toward some newly necessary meaning, do we assume the Holy Spirit is at work here, too? The Gospel of Mark is a much starker and less comforting book without its last twelve verses, which every reputable scholar agrees were added long after the original Gospel was composed. There are, as you know better than I, endless examples of this belated tinkering throughout the entire Bible. Must we pretzel our intelligences to allow for a Holy Spirit so committed to revision? Then again, I know from my own work as a poet that revision, when it's done rightly, is an echo of inspiration, diminished in its intensity but still ineluctably attached to its source.

When I think of what makes scripture sacred, I can think only of the many and various human lives through which it has passed and that have passed through it. There were Christians before there was a New Testament (though perhaps it's misleading to call them "Christians"?). There were believers before there was any Bible at all. And even when there was a decided Bible, for hundreds of years the great majority of people had no access to it. Sacredness is not a quality inherent to scripture, any more than it is inherent to nature. It is activated by our engagement with it, though that makes it seem too one-sided, as both scripture and nature enable that kind of engagement. Reality itself is, at its most basic level, pure contingency until we turn our attention to it. Why should scripture be different from the atoms of which it's made? In Philip Larkin's great poem "Church Going," the unbelieving speaker wonders why he so often stops to visit old churches. Here's how the poem ends:

A serious house on serious earth it is,
In whose blent air all our compulsions meet,
Are recognized, and robed as destinies.
And that much can never be obsolete,
Since someone will forever be surprising
A hunger in himself to be more serious,
And gravitating with it to this ground,
Which, he once heard, was proper to grow wise in,
If only that so many dead lie round.

A dim vision? I don't think so, because it's so hard-won. (Read Larkin's "Aubade" if you want to see the kind of mind from which "Church Going" was wrested.) The great achievement of modern art was to sacralize ordinary experience (Charles Taylor, *A Secular Age*). What got lost was any feel for, much less devotion to, *extraordinary* experience, the kinds of experiences the Bible describes, the fugitive and visionary glimpses of which the church is both elegy and testament. What I so loved about Jon Fosse's *Septology* was that it seemed, after all the flailings of postmodernism, like such a clear advance beyond modernism, faithful both to the sacred nature of ordinary life (think of how much of that book is devoted to Asle's daily, mundane actions) *and* to the realm of rapture and grace that underlies, is implicit within, the ordinary, the timeless gleam that makes, if we will see it, time's light such a vast and meaning thing.

It occurs to me how readily many people, maybe most contemporary intellectuals, would dispute that last sentence. Yesterday I listened to a podcast with Geoffrey Hinton, usually referred to as the "godfather of AI." Hinton has become alarmed that the technology to which he has devoted his life may actually end human life. He seems genuinely terrified by this, but near the end of the interview he said something that made me wonder why. In trying to convince the reporter that his (the reporter's) writing process was indistinguishable from the workings of AI, Hinton declared that humans are, in the end, simply machines and that any sense of self-consciousness we have is an illusion. (A "benign user illusion" is how the cognitive scientist Daniel Dennett describes it.) I think this vision underlies many intellectuals' philosophies of existence, even if they don't fully articulate it. The thing is, no one *lives* this way. No one says "I love you" to their spouse or child winkingly, as it were, simultaneously acknowledging the neurons to which they are unconsciously enslaved. If Hinton really believes there's no difference between our minds and the "minds" of AI, then what difference does it make if the latter displace us? If one's philosophy of life is at odds with the way they live that life, it seems obvious that one of those things is an error. The weight on one side here—toward ordinary life, life as people actually live it—doesn't necessarily prove the falseness of the philosophy, but it ought to at least check one's confidence in declaring the truth of materialism.

And this brings me, inevitably, to Jesus. What do I make of his teachings? Probably not enough. What would it look like if we really took him to be the exemplar our lessons and liturgies make him out to be? You mentioned a couple of letters back your disquiet at the thought of relinquishing parental control to Jesus, giving little Mira over to a diet of dust and turned cheeks. (How anyone ever squeezed a prosperity gospel out of that rocky doctrine is beyond me.) But even at the most basic levels, it seems to me that most Christians (though not all) become suddenly very adept at metaphorical understandings when confronted with the starkness of Jesus's teachings. Eschew all wealth and practice a kind of bare-bones communism within a community of believers? Surely he meant this *spiritually*, right? Or that bit about "hating" our loved ones, even our very selves, as the price to closeness with Christ, he can't actually *mean* that, can he? Surely he means that in loving my loved ones I must be conscious of loving Christ in them; so long as I keep this in mind, keep each in its proper order, I can have both, Christ and Danielle.

Maybe so. There's always a way to dodge the spotlight of these teachings with inventive interpretations. But what if Jesus really was that absolute? What if we are meant to take him at his word?

The difficulty, of course, is that some of the parables and teachings *are* metaphors, and sometimes their meanings are not at all clear. As it happens, for the past two weeks I've gone to Mass with Danielle, and the homilies have focused, first, on the parable of the virgins who didn't have oil for their lamps, and then on the parable of the servant who buried his "talent." The priest gave a brilliant, moving, and understated homily about the first parable, which he said had troubled him for forty years: How could he worship a God so officious and unforgiving? (Why not punish the virgins with the oil, who so sneeringly refused to share?) He said that he'd finally concluded that the virgins' chief sin was not in their failure to fulfill the terms of the law (a sin, but not a damnable one), and not in their lack of industry and effort (what oil merchant would be open at midnight?—it was a fool's errand). No, the chief sin lay in their lack of patience and trust. What might have happened had they simply waited, welcomed the bridegroom, and thrown themselves upon his mercy? Maybe *that*, for us, is the point of the parable: It is our *hearts* that must be ready, however unprepared we are in terms of the "law" (which, for our purposes, might include things like deciding whether or not the Bible is "sacred" and what it has to do with how we live our lives).

A bit of a stretch, maybe, but I found it moving, especially because it was so obvious that this priest really had been wrestling with this one story for forty years, waiting for it to disclose a meaning—*a* meaning, not *the* meaning—to him. He has lived out the patience that is missing in the story.

The next one—the parable of the talents—is an even tougher nut. A rich landowner goes away for a while and tasks his servants to take care of his "talents" (which, despite all of the sermons to the contrary, cannot mean "gifts"; this dual meaning is not in the original). Everyone proves to be a savvy investor except for the poor sod who, knowing his master to be a brutal and rapacious man, "reaping where thou has not sown, and gathering where thou hast not strawed," buries his portion for safekeeping. The master doesn't dispute the servant's characterization of him.

Indeed, he embraces it, and says that the very knowledge ought to have stoked the servant's mercenary cunning. The servant loses not only his one talent but his life.

The priest had a much more difficult time with this one and eventually just muttered, "If this is the God I've been serving my whole life, I want nothing more to do with him. I'm done." (He is admirably candid, this priest.) The tacit admission was that there are things in the Bible that are simply . . . wrong. And part of reading the Bible correctly is knowing what to jettison. This parable doesn't align with any other depiction of God that Jesus provides, and it is wildly out of keeping with everything else that Jesus teaches. Interpreting "talents" as "gifts" has for centuries softened and made palatable the moral, and if one accepts that the Holy Spirit is active in revisions, then she's probably waving her wand over mistranslations as well. But these explanations are pretty hard to swallow, and even then the parable sits there like a shard of glass in the gut. I have heard people say that the talents represent God's word as Jesus has passed it to the disciples, thereby enjoining them—and by extension us—to make something of what we have been given. The parable seems a crude and prickly vehicle for this rather simple advice, and the interpretation a last-ditch effort to avoid internalizing its essential indigestibility.

I keep thinking about what you said a while ago about our culture knowing God better than we know Jesus, the paradox of this, since Jesus, at least according to theologians like Barth, is the *only* thing we can know about God. I have no "relationship with Christ" in the sense that evangelicals use that phrase, rarely pray to him and find the character that comes across in the Gospels pretty remote and rebarbative. But then I think of the man who was so gentle with the woman at the well or the woman who touched the hem of his robe. I think of him scandalously washing the feet of his disciples, scandalously (and yet so movingly) calling out to the God who seemed to have abandoned him. I think of the heroic composure with which he accepted his fate. And I want nothing more in life than to know this man, to have his presence in my heart, to be strong enough to stake my entire existence on the reality of his.

Chris

DECEMBER 24

Dear Chris,

I feel at a disadvantage discussing death with you. You know death more intimately than I do, having looked into its face more than once and each time for more than a moment. I never have. Not my own death, at least. But whether death's shadow is short or long, we all live under it. Is death one of the things to which I say "no"? you ask.

Some people think that we must say "no" to death because anything that the sharp edge of death's scythe is destined to touch can be no more significant than a flower of the field. Others believe that we must say "yes" to death to say "yes" to life, that death defines life as its edge, that meaning and liveliness would drain out of life without such end. I don't like either option. I like least of all Socrates's take on death. His last words, after the poison he had taken had started to take effect, were to instruct his friend, Crito, "We owe a cock to Asclepius." Asclepius was the god of healing, and Socrates implied that death was about to heal him of the disease called life. (Some interpreters argue that Plato might have invented the scene and that Socrates would never have said anything of the sort. At the end of *The Joyful Science*, Nietzsche reported it as Socratic, but was puzzled about how a man so full of life as Socrates could have thought of life as disease.)

As I see it, "yes" to life takes care of the "no" to death—by complexifying the "no" as well, by making one say a kind of "no" that includes a confident "yes." We live toward death. When the last grain of sand falls into the bottom ampule through the throat of the hourglass, life is over. The image misleads us, though, to think that what is in the top ampule is ours, that passage of time and death take away what by nature belongs to us. I believe that life is given to us afresh every moment we are alive. We live toward death as those who are suspended over nothingness all along; even our liveliest moments could have not been. How long will God keep nothingness from swallowing us? Contingent as we are, we live because a "no" to death—our own "no" and God's—in the form of "yes" to life, is being enacted across the entire span of our life.

"The present form of this world is passing away," writes the apostle Paul. Death is part of the present form of the world's life, natural to it, as you note. But is the end of the present form of my life also the end of any form of my life? Like Bertrand

Russell, I know that when I die I shall rot. That, too, is what my parents signed me up for when they conceived me. That's what I *know*. What I *hope for*, though, is that as I rot I shall be raised to everlasting life. Death is "the end of a prelude to a symphony of which we only have a vague inkling of hope," wrote Abraham Heschel. In dispute with Sadducees who, unlike Pharisees, did not believe in life after death, Jesus quoted the words with which God self-identified to Moses from the burning bush: "I am the God . . . of Abraham, the God of Isaac, and the God of Jacob." Jesus drew a surprising conclusion from the quote: "Now he is God not of the dead, but of the living; for to him all of them are alive." For me, this is the most compelling argument for life after death, expressed in hypotheticals. *If* God is not dead and *if* God is not the God of the dead but of the living and *if* God is committed to all of us as God is to Abraham's progeny, we will always be alive to God.

I love your cypress, fierce and frigid winds, all messengers of the last icy blast, and its own resistances to them twisting it into stunning shape and making it thrive. I love it, though I cannot make myself want this for any of my children. I know an old cypress, still holding, barely, on to the cliff, waiting for the last blast. On April 11 this year, three days after he turned ninety-seven, he addressed a group of friends who came to celebrate his life:

> Every morning I am amazed that I am still here . . . To die means to let go. I am preparing myself for this. To die means to give one's life over to God. I am preparing myself for that, too. The raising to eternal life is my hope in life and in death. The eternal life will also be lived. This is the life of God's new creation. Death is like a birthday to new life in God's kingdom. Every morning of every new day that hope gives me new courage to live. But I did not invite you here to ponder things with me but to rejoice with me. Let us toast to life—here and there!

These are Moltmann's words, as you have likely guessed. He is about to step onto the bridge between the two forms of life, and he is celebrating both. "In my end is my beginning," he likes to say, quoting the last line of T. S. Eliot's "East Coker." The ground of his hope? "On the basis of the resurrection of Christ," he stated in the same address, "I believe in the resurrection to the eternal life at the hour of our death."

In an earlier letter you mentioned Tomáš Halík's view that

the crucifixion and the resurrection of Jesus Christ are not two acts of a drama, a triumph of life over death, but a single act. "The resurrection *interprets* the crucifixion," you wrote. This is a common view in modern protestant theology. Everything Jesus came to do was done when he breathed his last; the story of the resurrection helps us see the crucifixion rightly. I could never bring myself to embrace the theory, the sparkly lipstick on the impotence and futility of a life of love in the face of murderous political tyranny and death. I very much agree, though, that resurrection is not "*merely* a 'happy ending.'" It is a confirmation that the future belongs to just the kind of love Jesus enacted on the cross. That's how I read *Carmen Christi*, too. The glorification of Jesus, who, as God's equal, took the form of a slave and died the most shameful death, is the glorification of this humble act of self-decentering love. Resurrection is both the interpretation of the cross and the raising of the crucified.

In that same letter, you noted that imagination—the hope of resurrection—"is powerless in the face of extreme suffering." You would know better than I. And even had I suffered as much as you have, my experience with hope would have been my own and needn't be yours. In my more ordinary suffering, the hope of resurrection has had some power. There is a long tradition of philosophical and religious thinking, exemplified in Pseudo-Dionysius, according to which lovers are gradually transformed into the objects of their love. In his *Lectures on Romans*, Luther applied that idea to hope. The "soul is more where it loves than where it lives," wrote Bernard of Clairvaux; the soul "resides in that which it does not see, that is, in hope," Luther echoed him. As love transforms the lover into the beloved, so "hope changes the one who hopes into what is hoped for." I *am* my love and my hope. I hope, though, always for that which is not seen, for the unknown, most so when I hope for eternal life. Vague inkling of glorious hope, more a confident trust than an expectation of the specific outcome.

Lots of Bible in this letter, and that just after you pushed against relying much on it—and not for the first time in our correspondence. You ask, what makes a book "sacred" in which a timid servant, paralyzed by a harsh master, returns to the master the entire sum with which he was entrusted and the master throws him "into the outer darkness, where there will be weeping and gnashing of teeth" for being "wicked and lazy"!? Here is an example of my own to underscore your point. Ever since I read Bertrand Russell's "Why I Am Not a Christian" as a teenager, I could not but think that there is something morally wrong with a hungry Jesus cursing a fig tree even though, as the text explicitly states, "it was not the season for figs." What is "sacred" about the book in which those portrayed as moral exemplars behave in what seem to us morally repugnant ways? Why should we elevate the Good Book, as interpreted by ancient theologians, above the "book of nature"? Why not instead use the "book of nature," illuminated so ably by the sciences, as the lens through which to read the Good Book? And why contrast "sacred" to "ordinary"—the Bible and, say, poetry—rather than finding sacredness in the ordinary?

I am with you in the desire to expand the domain of the sacred, to celebrate the sacred in the ordinary, even if only as a sliver of light in the darkness, as *Septology*'s Asle does in his paintings. The last book of the Bible does, in fact, much more than identify traces of the sacred in the ordinary. It imagines the *entirety* of the ordinary as sacred. In the last two chapters of the book of Revelation, there is a vision of the New Jerusalem descended from heaven to earth. If you take it literally, as many do, it is completely phantasmagorical, as if Salvador Dali on psychedelics had painted it. ("I don't take drugs, I am a drug," I remember reading that he said.) If you read the vision symbolically and look for the origin of its strangely amalgamated images in the Hebrew Bible, a world of extraordinary meaning opens up. The city does not have a temple as any ancient city would. The entire city, cubic in shape, is imagined as the "holy of holies," the most sacred place in the Hebrew temple, the earthly throne of God. And what is the temple in which this planetary holy of holies is located? God is the temple. The entire city is in God and God is in the entire city. Ordinary things in creation are as sacred as anything in creation could be. The end of the Bible fits its beginning. For the Bible starts with creation that contains no line demarcating sacred spaces from ordinary. Scholars like Jon Levenson argue that in Genesis 1 the creation itself is portrayed as a temple. Others note that the Garden of Eden in Genesis 2 has aspects that mark it as a temple, too.

I am happy to bridge the sacred and the ordinary, to blur their boundaries, and experience the ordinary as sacred. Why then do I consider the Bible a "sacred" book? Why don't I give priority to the book of nature, give primacy to the natural sciences? In many domains I do just that. I don't go to consult the Bible about the history of the cosmos, of our own planet and all that is in it. I go to the sciences, to the stunning achievements of modern *explanatory reason* that tells a 13.8-billion-years-long story and connects the clicking of my keyboard as I write this to the Big Bang. Similarly, I don't go to the Bible if I want to find out how to get from any point A to point B. As you did when you were cured of cancer through experimental treatment, I seek to avail myself of all the achievements of modern *instrumental reason*. It may seem that I have just made God redundant. I haven't. Theology has much to say about God's and humans' relation to each other and the rest of reality, which takes me to the importance of the Bible.

When I ask "What kind of life should I live?" or "What kind of life is worthy of our shared humanity?" explanatory and instrumental reason are of limited use. It is not in the nature of these intellectual endeavors to answer the question of purpose and moral obligation. Though they can advise me how to reach easier this or that moral goal that I have, they cannot tell me what moral goals or human purposes I *should* make my own. Explanatory and instrumental reason cannot give me the "tables of value" (Nietzsche) or "hypergoods" (Taylor)—those convictions on the basis of which I can judge something as humane or not, morally worthy of pursuit or not. (Along with many others, Nietzsche thought otherwise, though I think that he was mistaken.)

Where should I go for the tables of value? One option is just to improvise, to look for some kind of personal authenticity in my endeavors or to pursue what strikes me as right at the moment. As Tara Isabella Burton has argued in *Strange Rights* and *Self-Made*, many today are choosing some such improvisational path. To me, the option feels like despair glitzing itself up into meaning. Life is too short, pulled in too many different directions all at once, too precious to improvise living it. I need a guide—and patience to live myself into the wisdom of a path. Potential guides are those in the history of humanity who have thought a great deal about meaning and purpose, and whose ideas have been embraced, lived, and refined over the centuries. They may be philosophers (like Socrates, Kant, or Mill), religious figures (like Moses, Jesus, or Muhammad), or those who straddle what we generally call philosophy and religion (like Confucius or the Buddha).

As a teenager, I found a guide in Jesus Christ, in his story within the story of God's dealings with Israel and the world, which is where the Bible and its "sacredness" comes in for me. The only way to get to Jesus Christ and that larger story is through the Bible, directly or indirectly. The Bible is a Christ-bearer—and it acquires its sacredness from him, the Holy One in flesh. As to the

Hebrew Bible, I find that even apart from its relation to Christ, it speaks to me like no other book does. As I was writing *The Home of God*, I read Exodus with enough care to be able to write two chapters on it. Its moral ambiguity notwithstanding—or, perhaps, just because of its moral ambiguity—I experienced it as extraordinary in so many ways, like being the source of much of Western political thinking. Like the Psalms, Job, or the prophet Isaiah, it spoke to me with a voice that called me back to myself, drawing me into my own fullness.

For me, the Bible is the finger pointing toward Jesus Christ, a very human finger! Christian theologians have only rarely believed that God dictated the Bible the way Muslims believe that God dictated the Qur'an. I don't even think of the inspiration of the Bible the way you experience inspiration in writing poetry with you-as-Chris set aside for something else to write through you. I leave a lot of room for omissions and additions, for revisions and embellishments. Just look at the Gospels—four renderings of the story of Christ with distinct emphases and with some details that are impossible to harmonize. I feel no need to pretzel my intelligence "to allow a Holy Spirit so committed to revision." Evangelists and apostles are telling and applying the story of Christ from their perspective and for the needs of their audiences. The texts are more like simple sermons than like learned treatises or great literary works. The Bible is "great" and "sacred" because, in its own undistinguished and seemingly unwise way, it bears witness to Christ—which is what the apostle Paul said of his own sermons. Nicholas Wolterstorff, who taught at Yale Divinity School before you came, has written a very learned philosophical treatise propounding the theory that God appropriated the texts of biblical writers as God's own speech.

What do I do with actions and teachings in the Bible that I find morally wrong—for instance, the one you mentioned that seems to demand that I hate Jessica. I interpret it in the context of the entire teaching of Jesus, like the one where he elevates love of neighbor to almost the same status as love for God: In importance, the second great commandment is, he says, "like unto" the first. If anybody is my neighbor, she is. Other actions and teachings I situate in their own cultural context, and if I still find them problematic, I park them where they are not in the way—with openness that my judgment, though firm, could prove not to be final. It did happen in fact that I came to see wisdom in a teaching where before I could only see moral harm, for instance, in the hard saying of Jesus to which you refer:

"Whoever comes to me and does not hate father and mother, wife and children, brothers and sisters, yes, and even life itself, cannot be my disciple." I take "hate" to be hyperbolic and to state with force the order of priorities in Jesus's disciples' lives: God alone is to be loved with all of one's powers, and love for God—love for Love—is above love for any worldly good, even love of one's life itself. (So something like what you called a hierarchy of loves.) That cursed fig-tree passage, though, has been parked for more than half a century now, and when I recently reread it during our Wednesday Bible reading at the Yale Center for Faith and Culture, I got strangely animated, even angry. The passage about the slaughter of the worshippers of the golden calf in Exodus, Moses's command to the sons of Levi to go "throughout the camp, and each of you kill your brother, your friend, and your neighbor," remains parked, too.

You urge reading the Bible with greater freedom than most theologians do, more like we read literary works. I largely agree. You mention exegetical debates about "is" in the eucharistic phrase "This is my body" as an example of the hollowness and contentiousness of readings with doctrinal formulations in view. On the face of it, the debate does seem preposterous. And yet, protracted debates about the minutiae of Biblical texts are rarely about nothing. The way we understand the verb "is" in that phrase is tied to the way we understand how God relates to creation, and that in turn has bearing on how we understand the character and the purposes of human life. In the Bible, ontological claims are of existential import. If I took the Bible to be one among many resources for free improvisation of life, I would play with it to see what meanings might emerge that would be useful or simply clever. But how can I "play" with the text that for me has the authority of the bearer of the moral measure of my life—and of my world? I mean this as a serious question.

This measure of my life I experience as a broad place to be. When my mother was in her late teens after WWII, and the communists had just come to power, she was riding on a train and quietly reading her Bible. Two plain clothes policemen came into the compartment, confiscated the Bible, and took her off the train at the next station. They interrogated her for no greater crime than reading the Bible. The holy book was subversive; reading it relativized the power of the regime. This is how the Bible felt to me when I started reading it in my teens—and this is how it still feels, wild and not pious at all. I love it for that.

I don't want to domesticate it, cut it down to the measure of dominant cultural or countercultural sensibilities.

I found what you wrote about Jesus in your last letter—and also in the earlier one about union with Christ in suffering and the radiance which that union gave to the world—deeply moving. I want to know more, especially about that radiance.

Miroslav

JANUARY 19

Dear Miroslav,

When you say that you respond to the Bible more deeply than any other book, my chief feeling is . . . jealousy. I sometimes feel I'm never *further* from God than when I'm reading the Bible, which makes me resent the way scripture is made into a kind of entry ticket for Christianity, especially by Protestants. If I followed your method, I'd have to "park" something on just about every page.

An example. I have recently been reading Acts (hope springs eternal!). At one point, after Paul has healed several people, the focus shifts to his disciples, who use various articles of Paul's clothing to perform their own healings. This doesn't sit right with a sudden demon, who protests, from within the person in whom he resides, that he knows Jesus and Paul but not these schmucks and proceeds to not only scourge them but to strip them naked (?) and drive them into the streets. Then it's back to Paul, whose sermon is interrupted by a man named Eutychus, who is apparently so bored that he plunges out of a window to his death. Paul is undeterred. He goes downstairs, quickly brings Eutychus back to life, and continues with his sermon. This all happens in two or three pages. Spiritless, confused, frustrated with my own "irritable reaching after fact and reason," I opened another book beside me and read—

> One thing does not exist: Oblivion.
> God saves the metal and he saves the dross.
> And his prophetic memory guards from loss
> The moons to come, and those of evenings gone.
>
> —Jorge Luis Borges,
> "Everness," translated by
> Richard Wilbur

This lifted me out of myself, into myself, my mind suddenly charged with that fusion of thought and feeling I associate with the deepest truth. (*Prophetic* memory. This is what it means to think of—to *feel*—hope as retroactive as well as prospective. Not to be freed from time, but to be freed from its limiting linearity, which is a property not of time but of our vision.)

How much of that passage from Acts would you "park"? Do you simply accept the supernatural occurrences as vestiges of another time and treat the whole thing as a series of parables/

metaphors that we are meant to interpret for our own lives? How do you understand Paul's resurrection of Eutychus, which, besides being hard to swallow in itself, might even be seen to diminish, even to cheapen, the resurrection that occurred a few years earlier, upon which the whole Christian faith is founded? Perhaps some people assume that Eutychus was simply wounded and Paul nursed him back to consciousness, but that's not what the text says. And perhaps Jesus's resurrection is an altogether different kind of event, inaugurating a different kind of life rather than simply restoration to the one we know. But I feel some degree of absurdity in trying to discriminate between *kinds* of resurrection.

I feel I still don't know *how* to read the Bible—the New Testament at least. The Old Testament is much clearer in terms of genre. Thinking of Adam, Eve, Noah, Job, etc. as historical figures is simply a literary naivete. Obviously there's history in the Old Testament, but the main stories are so clearly parables and myths (which, of course, doesn't for a second mean they are *untrue*). The New Testament is a different animal. There are fictional techniques employed in the Gospels, as when Jesus goes off to pray alone and we are made privy to his internal thoughts. That scene with Eutychus reads like fiction to me, even broad comedy, and Luke is definitely the most literary and self-aware of the Synoptic Gospel writers. What do these moments—and, of course, there are others—teach us about how to read the texts as a whole? What is history and what is fiction? How and where do you draw the line, and how do you fit all this into your faith—and not simply the supernatural content but other affronts to one's sense of dignity and justice, like Paul's clear-cut injunctions for women to be subordinate to men?

I don't think it's true that we can come to Jesus only through the Bible. As I said in my last letter, there were many Christians before there was a Bible. And there are many Christians now who know nothing of the Bible. You mention that Tara Isabella Burton book. In it, she notes the results of a study revealing that half of the Americans who call themselves Christians can't name the four Gospels. Half! Even given my Biblical resistance, I find this depressing. (Don't get me wrong: I think the Bible is extremely important and very definitely *can be* sacred. Much of it is deeply embedded in, and essential to, my own spiritual life.) But I don't think it follows that these people are not Christians. I'm sure you don't either. I know many people for whom the Bible is a great stumbling block to their faith. In some instances, they have come to Christianity later in life, usually after some intense experience of joy or loss. They read religious literature, they seek out people of faith to talk to, and slowly they find themselves forging a faith—find themselves being reforged by faith. Inevitably they try to read the Bible, and inevitably it is a crushing experience. I have to believe *this*? they wonder. Others have been raised in Evangelical households like me, and the faith they've retained, remade, salvaged is very different from that in which they were raised. But they're unable to free themselves completely from the Bible as be-all. It's like a stuck anchor for a boat that's ready to sail.

Here's a thought experiment. What might Jesus make of our modern (meaning post-Reformation) obsession with the New Testament? He never wrote a word, of course, unless you count the time he mysteriously scribbled in the dust. He also said, "My words will last forever," a statement that seems far more profound than merely predicting the Gospels. It seems more likely he was saying that, because of his life, the Word is now burned into the word, eternity into reality. His life will survive in the things people say to one another, the stories they pass down about God walking among us and sharing our suffering. It will also survive in the things not said to one another, in the fluent silences of a world now charged and changed with the grandeur of God. Even that act of writing in the dust is instructive. The *one* time Jesus engages in the act of writing he chooses to write something that not only is not recorded but is literally inscribed in reality itself, on and into the very earth. It seems triumphantly perishable, akin to the uncanny feeling of transcendence that emanates off of this runic little secular scripture:

The Poem

I think there is no light in the world
but the world.

And I think there is light.

—George Oppen

Just before I sat down to write this letter I read this sentence from the talented and too-early deceased Lucy Grealy: "It's when I read people writing about the Bible that I feel most alien from religion; and also when I feel the most sorry for us all." At first I nodded with a sense of solidarity, but a second later I thought: *Maybe she's talking about me.* Drawing lines between fact and fiction, nitpicking first-century social expectations, agonizing over what this haphazard collection of miscellaneous texts has to do with the burn of being I find in the life of Christ. This is what I mean by not knowing how to read the Bible. Maybe I should just relax and let my method—hold hard to what inspires, throw away the rest—suffice. But clearly I'm not able to do that.

I'm not happy with this letter. We embarked upon this project because we wanted to speak honestly about faith, to help each other clarify where we stand at this point in our lives. Arguing about the Bible makes me feel legalistic and small. Part of Christianity's appeal for me—a warrant to its truth, in fact—is its flagrant insult to common sense. A god that supersedes space and time, that conceived of these things? A god who in some marvelous, mysterious act of self-parturition sends himself to dwell among men? Absurd! Yet it accords with the reality I feel myself, at rare moments, to inhabit. It helps me to understand suffering, and joy, and being itself.

But this affront occurs at a cosmological level. When the insults get closer to home, in my face, so to speak (Eutychus!), I feel that this grand symmetry is being not only violated but vulgarized. I have been part of communities that spoke in tongues and practiced healings, that interpreted every coincidence as evidence of answered prayers. I suspect that's what we're seeing in the Acts and the letters of Paul. If I can read that Eutychus passage as a rare bit of humor in the New Testament, a gentle mockery of Paul's bullheaded self-assurance, then I love it. If I have to consent to it as history, then I'm out.

Does this mean the Bible is "merely" literature? No. It has meant too much, in too many lives, to suggest that (and in any event much of it wouldn't qualify as literature). And I also realize that there is some special quality to this text, that the right attention can release meanings that come from the very heart of God. But God is so much larger than this book, and has given us so many other ways to know him. "That's not biblical" is the line Evangelicals use to shut down any insight with which they are uncomfortable. I heard it yesterday on a podcast when someone was denying the reality of near-death (or even post-death) experiences: "That's not biblical." *Who cares*, I wanted to shout at the radio. Thinking of God like this—thinking of the *Bible* like this—is like believing you're in the middle of the Sahara when you're really just playing in a sandbox.

Chris

FEBRUARY 29

Dear Chris,

I agree with most of what you wrote in your last letter. God is greater than the Bible, and God can speak through any means, even through a dead dog, as Karl Barth is reported to have said. People can come to faith and live lives of devotion to God and love of neighbor without ever touching the Bible. And, yes, the Bible is a strange book, for some an obstacle to spiritual life and only in rare cases the sole means of coming to faith. (I know of only one such case, a teen visual artist who grew up in an a-religious household, found an old Bible, read in it, and came to my father's church to learn more.) And yet, all great spiritual masters of the Christian faith, only some of them theologians, were primarily interpreters of the Bible.

I think I get your puzzlement about reading the New Testament. Not great literature. The Hebrew Bible is a different matter, as you note; Jahweh is a strong character, as Harold Bloom would say. Take any Gospel or Epistle and compare it to, say, one of Plato's dialogues. No contest. As literary and intellectual achievements, Plato's dialogues are superior even to the best of Paul's letters. Like you, I am lifted into my own aesthetic and intellectual self when reading texts like Plato's *Symposium* or Borges's "Everness."

Speaking of that poem, you commented on its marvelous third line, on the phrase "prophetic memory," which names so deftly the overlapping of times in remembering. As I read the first stanza you quoted, I halted at the end of the second line: "God saves the metal and he saves the dross." *Aesthetically*, I was at one with myself, but existentially I felt like I was being pulled down into a morass. The God who keeps everything, the metal and the dross, and, presumably, the fire that separates the two!? The God who affirms it all and, like some divinized Nietzsche, says a sacred Yes to the entire cauldron of the churning world!? I can do without such a God. Still, the world would be poorer without Jorge Louis Borges and that poem.

Most of the New Testament is a collection of simple texts written for simple people. I love it for that. I love not so much the common, earthen vessel that it is, but the uncommon treasure that it holds. Which might explain why time stops when I *study* the Bible, but why I don't particularly like just to read it. Neither do I like to read most of the modern commentaries on the Bible. They are about the Bible, the earthen vessel, but most of them are not about what the Bible is about. Lucy Grealy may well have been talking about modern Bible commentators. They take me away from the treasure—and yet, they, too, can be a way to get back to it.

In my last letter, I wrote that for me the Bible is a finger pointed to Christ. The Monastery of St. Anthony's in Issenheim, France, has a marvelous altarpiece by Matthias Grünewald from the beginning of the sixteenth century. At its center is the crucifixion scene. To the right of the crucified Christ stands John the Baptist. A red camel hair cloak is draped around his shoulders and fastened to his body at the waist with a strange piece of leather tied in a knot. He is pointing his thin, outstretched, and illuminated index finger toward the Crucified while, in the other hand, holding an open book, the Hebrew Bible. Behind him, Grünewald has written, in large but muted red letters, the words John the Baptist himself said of Jesus: "He must increase, but I must decrease." Karl Barth had a replica of the painting in his office. When visitors came, he would tell them that he saw himself and his writings, voluminous and learned, in the figure of John the Baptist, just pointing to Christ. I think the Bible is John the Baptist, his finger. Not clad in the soft, refined robes of a great teacher; no figure sitting sunken in thought (Socrates) or holding a stylus (Plato); instead, an ascetic, whose diet was locusts and wild honey, pointing with an emaciated finger away from himself to the crucified God. Like ten-month-old babies, some of us look at the finger rather than at that to which the finger points.

You resist "having to consent" to taking reports of the dead miraculously returning to life as facts, to treating biblical stories as history. As you should. When it comes to Christian faith, forced consent is always false. Faith is a free act in which a person is, at least intentionally, at one with themselves; "one believes [better: trusts] with the heart," writes Paul. God isn't an archautocrat with an army of invisible interrogators extracting confessions and consents from unwilling humans on the pain of eternal suffering. In fact, at the heart of the Christian faith isn't *anything* we do—not our beliefs (against excessive reliance on which you have pushed—rightly—in these letters), not our trust (which I think is important but secondary), not even our love (which both of us celebrate, whether it takes the form of attentiveness or service). Who God is and what God does are at the center. The whole of Christian faith is summed up in a single phrase from the New Testament: "God is love." Not: "God loves," as if loving were one of many things, maybe even the most important thing, that God does. But: "God *is* love," so that nothing God does isn't love. Schopenhauer in *The World as Will and Representation*, and, after him, Nietzsche in *The Joyful Science*, liked to imagine our lives as little boats that sail in "the raging, boundless sea," which "rises up and casts down howling cliffs of waves." For both, this was a key image of life in a godless world. To embrace the claim that God is love is to make a wager on the conviction that the turbulent sea is enfolded in God's love and that God sleeps in the stern of every little boat—and when God awakes and commands the storm to be still, more often than not it is to help those who "have no faith."

Miroslav

PS. I can see how someone who denies life after death would sense "absurdity in trying to discriminate between two *kinds* of resurrection." For those who want to entertain the idea of life after death, the distinction between revivification and resurrection is crucial, an aspect of the distinction between "this life" and what the Nicene Creed calls "the life of the world to come." These are two different forms of life.

APRIL 17

Dear Miroslav,

God is love. This is my conception and deep intuition of God, too—until I read the Bible. Even in the New Testament there are passages that test this notion. The Old Testament sometimes obliterates it, or requires a radical enlargement of what one means by "love," which must come to include jealousy and prejudice and even wholesale slaughter. Did you ever read Jack Miles's "biography" of God? (We read his follow-up on Jesus for that Christ in Modern Literature class we taught.) His aim is to delineate the character of God as it emerges and "develops" (God is very changeable, according to Miles's reading) in the Tanakh. It's a brilliant book (and justly won the Pulitzer), but I remember being very disturbed by it. God comes across as needy, volatile, borderline psychotic at times. This wasn't the disturbing part. I've heard that version of the Old Testament God all my life. What disturbed me was how meticulously Miles hewed to the text, how *convincing* it was as exposition. I was just returning to Christianity then and mentioned my qualms to a minister, who counseled me to throw that book in the trash posthaste. Which I found even more disturbing.

I thought of Miles (and even reread parts of his book) when I went on a podcast with Marilynne a couple of weeks ago to talk about her new reading of Genesis, which is basically the opposite of Miles's. She argues that all of those troubling incidents actually *establish* the notion that God is love. All those people and creatures wiped out in the Flood? At least God saved someone, she says; at least God saw us as worth another try. Abraham's near sacrifice of Isaac? Tough for those two, yes, but the story modeled a form of propitiation that other tribes, locked in a law of child sacrifice, could now emulate. It ushered in a new era. These sound a little absurd baldly stated as I am doing, but Marilynne is Marilynne, and her readings have real force and authority. Noah is a character in a legend, she says. (She actually calls it a sacred history, but it seems to me she's reading the story as a legend.) We are *all* Noah, just as we are all also the people destroyed. (Not sure how to account for the animals.) This never happened, and it happens all the time, God rescuing us collectively and individually from our own propensity for self-destruction.

(An aside that I know will interest you: At one point the moderator asked us to speak about the deepest part of our faith, some bedrock belief that we found ourselves continually returning to, leaning on. I talked about my sense of the absolute connectedness of matter and mind, some ultimate reality and coherence of which we are given glimpses in our life and work but which also forever elude us. Predictable. Then Marilynne dropped what was for me a bomb. She said she was continually surprised and reassured by the ultimate *goodness* of humans, that this was where she saw the fact—I think she really does see it as a fact—of our having been made in God's image most directly. I was speechless. Still am, to some degree, though in the days after I found myself grateful that there was someone in the world—and not just any someone—who really believed this and had staked her whole life and work on that belief.)

At this point in my life, I'm not "convinced" by either Marilynne's or Miles's readings. They both seem to me novel and provocative ways of reading the Bible, and fairly irrelevant to my conception of God. It seems to me obvious that the story of Noah, just as the story of Job, presents real moral difficulties with regard to the "character" of God. But God is not a character. The Bible—like art, like nature—is littered with clues about God's nature, and human nature, and nature itself, but it's also—like art but unlike nature—filled with human error, wish-fulfillment, vanity, and outright manipulation. I do believe the Holy Spirit can lead us to a right relation with this book, but I'll never believe that this somewhat random assemblage of disparate texts is the result of divine guidance, or even that it's absolutely essential to the life of a Christian.

And yet, I read it just about every single day. Most mornings I wake and slam my qualms against that rock of unreality. (How struck I was—and helped—by your distinction between reading and studying the Bible!) And sometimes a little spark of truth emerges and begins to burn.

For instance: Last week I preached in Marquand for the first time in several years. (How much I have missed this, I realized the minute I stood at the podium and looked out at the faces of students and colleagues.) I think I told you on one of our walks that I have been reading Carlos Eire's book *They Flew: A History of the Impossible*, which focuses on the levitating saints of the sixteenth and seventeenth centuries. It's a work not only of rigorous scholarship but also of sensitive and provocative intelligence (and with, I suspect, a strong current of real faith in the background, though this is never made explicit). Carlos raises the question of a culture's epistemic reality and whether what we believe *can* happen has everything to do with what in fact *does* happen. Holy people were lifted into the air during their mystical raptures because that's what people expected holy people to do. It was a physical manifestation of a metaphysical reality, the body suspended between union with God (who was thought of as "up") and the ineluctable gravity of the flesh.

At the time, my morning rock-smashes were happening in the book of Jeremiah, where I came upon this startling spark (from God, through the mouth of the prophet): "I shall set my law within them, writing it on their hearts . . . No longer need they teach one another, neighbor or brother, to know the Lord; all of them, high and low alike, will know me." There's more, but you get the gist. A time will come when there is no need for churches, sermons, doctrines, or a Bible. No need for two old, bedraggled acolytes to write letters back and forth trying to figure out what they mean by "faith." (I think of the Stevie Smith poem we discussed earlier in which loving love without deifying it is the final fruition of the religious impulse.) The passage suggests an "epistemic reality" that is almost unimaginable, a faith that is coextensive with life itself, our minds so in tune with the world—with the world charged with God—that instinct, appetite, duty, and devotion all rhyme.

Almost unimaginable. I occasionally read those books in which famous physicists attempt to describe their work to a popular audience. You can spend an hour in one of these and feel like you've fallen through the looking glass. Quantum entanglement, the multiverse, electrons that not only respond to human perception but seem to actually intuit it (according to some of John Wheeler's experiments): Some of this stuff is as strange and rationally offensive as any levitating saint. In the sermon, using the passage from Jeremiah as a text, I wondered what it might mean for us if this knowledge were not simply a piece of information in a scientific journal but instead settled belief, part of how we saw our days. If reality is as fluid and shifting as some of these experiments suggest, and if human consciousness is in some way communing with the physical world in ways we don't understand, miracles might not even be miracles, or they would become something hitherto unimaginable. I think all the time about Psalm 148, which begins with the angels being enjoined to praise God but then swerves. Rocks must praise God, and rivers, and beasts—as if, three thousand years ago, some inspired poet had the sense that nature was sentient, which our modern science seems to be telling us is true.

It was that one verse from Jeremiah that sparked my sermon. It was that one moment of communion with the text that magnetized all the mental filings of my life into a single act of perception and, yes, praise. And I am well aware that this letter implicitly contradicts parts of my last letter, because, in case you couldn't tell, I find myself dangerously close to believing that St. Joseph of Cupertino really did fly around the skies of early seventeenth-century Italy.

What about you? Do you feel "trapped" by material reality? Do you feel our epistemic reality as a constriction? Have you ever, even briefly, had that reality violated, expanded, challenged? Personally, I mean.

I forgot to tell you one thing: I bracketed that sermon with a story of my grandfather, who on what he believed to be his deathbed was visited by a visible angel in his hospital room who said his name ("T. D.," which stood for, alas, Tom Dick rather than Thomas Richard) and then: "It's not time." My grandfather immediately began to improve and lived long enough to be in my life for eight years, by all accounts a transformed man.

Have you ever heard an angel, of whatever sort?

Chris

JUNE 2

Dear Chris,

A few days back on our walk, you asked me whether I pray, or perhaps it was how much I pray. I made some quick comment about my discomfort with prayer (of which I wrote early in our correspondence) and how I enjoy praying liturgically, saying the words of the good old, beautiful and deep, Book of Common Prayer. That's half the truth. Subconsciously, my mother's prayers define for me what it means to pray—a fierce wrestling with God until you've extorted a promise or gotten an explanation for the refusal, and from which you emerge with puffy, bloodshot eyes and a runny nose or, as in Jacob's case, with a wrenched hip. I have never wrestled with God, which is not to say that I don't admire Jacob and my mother for doing so. My prayers are different. I often carry a pocket cross, the one I almost lost at the airport. Sometimes I pray with prayer beads, reciting either the uncomfortable Jesus Prayer ("Lord Jesus Christ, Son of God, have mercy on me a sinner") or a version of the culminating line of St. Paul's great Epistle to the Romans: "From You, and through You, and to You are all things." I have a *komboskini*—an Orthodox knot prayer rope—hanging from the rearview mirror in my car, not as an amulet but as an identity reminder and an arrow of yearning. To me, prayer is, above all, about opening a space for God in the world, enabling God to "be at home in our time," to use a phrase from Abraham Heschel's essay on prayer. This way of praying has some affinity with the mystical tradition's "birth of God" in the soul (on which I draw mostly from the anonymous fourteenth-century text *Theologia Germanica*). Except that I don't pray for release from the world, but for God to come into the world, to feel at home in it. Creation is completed, enlivened, and elevated when God dwells in it.

You ended your last letter asking whether I'd experienced materiality, as ordinarily conceived, divinely "violated, expanded, challenged," whether I've ever seen or heard an angel. Someone very close to me, a person I can trust, had an experience like your grandfather's. I never did. I've never actually seen or experienced what I could, with some confidence, call a "miracle." It could be that my "epistemic reality" is constricted, to use Carlos Eire's phrase. I don't think, though, that God is absent from the world or asleep in it, like my father taking a Sunday nap after lunch in the middle of our bustling keeping room. God is active—the determining reality—in nonobvious ways. My own turning from resistance to God happened almost without me noticing it. In my mid-teens, I spent a good part of two summers traveling with a group of Swedish teenagers, all of them Christians, on a missionary vacation in Yugoslavia. My sole interest was in girls; that they were Swedish, which meant Western, was a bonus. At the end of the second summer, I made some vague commitment of faith, so vague that I remember almost nothing about it, except that it happened in Stockholm in a large tent, listening to a sermon by Stanley Sjöberg of which I understood at best 30 percent. The nonevent of my commitment seemed not to have made even a ripple in my soul, but when I came home my mother asked, "What happened to you?!" Her children were an open book to her, and she saw change where I experienced none. It defined my entire life. That's typical of how I experience God working. Always somewhere *behind* my consciousness and will. In moments of time as I live them, angels never call to me from heaven to prevent some calamity, as happened to Hagar, nor do they come to announce some great good news, as they did to Mary. But I do see them in my past, mostly vaguely.

They Flew is a fascinating read. Carlos Eire is a friend—we used to take walks together occasionally when I lived in Guilford—and I can attest that his faith is real. But I am not entirely sure what to make of the book. (I like most of what he writes, especially the autobiographical *Waiting for Snow in Havana.*) I am willing to grant that some saints likely levitated and bi-located, and if his other readers become willing to do the same, Carlos will have achieved his purpose, I think. But where exactly is God's agency in these phenomena? He seems to think of it in two ways. One is that *God made* the saints levitate and bi-locate, which is what the levitators and bi-locators themselves believed. The events are supernatural. The other way Carlos thinks of them is that we moderns, when we fail to believe and see the paranormal, are misreading the nature of the relationship between consciousness and material reality, that we are blind to the "hidden powers inherent in the human mind." The events are then natural—and have as much bearing upon how we think of God's active relation to the world as does my breathing. Or maybe it is a bit of both, supernatural and natural.

I have one worry about levitations in particular. Carlos, who is Catholic, would call it a Protestant worry. I get the point of an angel appearing to your grandfather or of Jesus miraculously feeding five thousand with two fish and five loaves, which, you can argue, is a particularly striking example of matter's multilocation. I don't get the point of levitation. It is fascinating—and it can be funny, as when Teresa of Avila senses, during a sermon on a feast day with dignitaries present, "that the Lord was about to do this to me," lays on the ground to resist it, and has her sisters hold her body down, unsuccessfully. Perhaps God uses special effects to keep our interest (though, according to sworn witnesses, the devil is producing them, too, and equally well, as Carlos reports). My problem may be that I am not into special effects, neither in movies nor in religion. All their dazzle makes me quickly yawn; I feel like a crow, attracted to a shiny object, and soon start to miss the depth, earthiness, and temporality of life. I find an ordinary human face much more interesting—any face that a scalpel blade and makeup haven't made into a special effect.

Jack Miles is a wonderful writer; no yawns reading him. When it comes to writing about God as a developing character, though, I am with Robert Alter:

> There is little to be gained, I think, by conceiving the biblical God, as Harold Bloom does, as a human character—petulant, headstrong, arbitrary, impulsive, or whatever. The repeated point of biblical writers is that we cannot make sense of God in human terms.

I take this Alter quote from Miles's book. What is his main justification for disagreeing with Alter? "One of the very earliest statements any biblical writer makes about God" is that humans were created in God's image! But you cannot flip "Humans are made in the image of God" to "God is rendered in the image of humans," as Miles implies. God is the creator; humans are creatures.

Be that as it may, the larger point Miles makes still stands and is important for our exchange about the defining attributes of God. The character of God clearly shifts or develops throughout the Bible. For anyone, though, who actually believes in the one God, creator of all that is seen and unseen, what develops is not so much God as God's relation to humans and human conceptions of God. God cannot appear to humans in unmediated divine reality. All accounts of God are linguistically, psychologically, and socially inflected by the culture of a given time and place; as human cultures change, humans' sense of God will partly change as well, at times significantly. More significantly, God's relation to humans changes. A good example is a shift from collective to individual human responsibility. In Exodus, God speaks of "visiting the iniquity of the parents upon the children"; in Ezekiel, God says that "a child shall not suffer for the iniquity of a parent." God *abrogated* in Ezekiel the principle God established in Exodus.

I was about to write to you that I am up to my eyeballs in Schopenhauer's metaphysical grumpiness and could not yet take time to read Marilynne's controversial take on the Flood in *Reading Genesis*. But then it dawned on me that there is a connection between the God of the Flood and the paradigmatic philosophical pessimist. The foundation of his pessimist creed is that the nonbeing of the world—of all living things and, above all, humans—would be better than its being. Schopenhauer's main work, *The World as Will and Representation*, culminates in a redemption of sorts: The blind Will, at the core of everything and the source of the world's suffering, negates itself. The last sentence of the book reads, "For those in whom the will has turned and negated itself, this world of ours which is so very real with all its suns and galaxies is—*nothing*." Now, is not the God who responds to the sorry state of humanity with "I am sorry that I have made them" a philosophical pessimist? Worse, a pessimistic dictator, who unleashes a cataclysm to bring about the better state of humanity's nonbeing?! Submerged underwater, the whole world comes to resemble the chaotic state before creation, when "a wind from God swept over the face of the waters." This made me want to see whether Marilynne offers any comfort. I was taken; I found it more compelling than anything I've read on the topic.

As you note, the key to her interpretation is the claim that Genesis 6–9 does not purport to give an account of what actually happened; it tells a fictional story. As I read the text, nudged by Marilynne's interpretation, we are in a hypothetical situation in which humans are made to appear as evil as they possibly can be. It is not just that their "wickedness was great." In a massive hyperbole, we read that "every inclination of the thoughts of their hearts was only evil continually." That's worse than every human being turning into a Lamech determined to avenge himself, for every slight, seventy-sevenfold! That's every human being rotten to the core. Kant's "radical evil" is the mere naughtiness of a child compared to this. The Flood destroys utterly corrupt humans, which we all potentially are but none can in fact become, though, to name just one example of actual corruption: How do you morally assess creators, sellers, and consumers who, to save a few dollars on a thousand-dollar item, send little children into the bowels of the earth, and do so without a second thought? I am resisting the temptation to say that such human beings *deserve* not to exist. Our mobile phones are real and the description of how they came to be is factual; the story of the Flood is *imagined* and human rottenness to the core as well. Why? To make a crucial point.

When the waters recede, God makes an everlasting covenant with humanity and all living beings: There will never again be such destruction. You might think that God would make such a solemn promise with the expectation that Noah and his descendants would act differently from how humans did before the Flood. Not so. No conditions are attached to the covenant; no behavioral ifs accompany it. The covenant is unconditional, and that not merely despite the evil God foresees that humans will do, but *because* of it: "The Lord said in his heart, 'I will never again curse the ground because of humankind, for the inclination of the human heart is evil from youth; nor will I ever again destroy every living creature as I have done.'" The reason human beings deserve the Flood becomes the reason why God promises not to send it; exactly that which ought to make humans forfeit the right to existence elicits God's mercy and occasions affirmation of God's everlasting faithfulness. God's declaration of unconditional love to the entire humanity is the surprising point of the story of the Flood. It takes unconditional love to lead into goodness the creatures prone to wickedness. In *Judaism Is About Love*, Shai Held makes a similar point about the relation between Genesis 6 and 8 and concludes: "God has decided to remain faithful to us, come what may." Does the interpretation feel a bit forced? It does. But the alternatives I know or can think of don't strike me as better.

It turns out that God is not a pessimist at all—and not because God lives in blissful ignorance, viewing the world as if it were some cheery spectacle. (Schopenhauer, who made this point, used the phrase "peep show," but today peep show means something different than in his time.) God isn't a pessimist because the goodness of the bare existence of the doer of even the worst deeds is inexpungible. And because God's love for creatures is predicated not on creatures' moral worth but on the character of God's very being.

There are passages in the Bible—both in the Torah and in the New Testament—that I cannot square with the claim that God is love, and yet I think that one can responsibly claim the entire Christian faith rests on it. (In a way, in *Judaism Is About Love*, Shai Held shows how the same is true of Judaism!) My own existential *credo*, my own "on this I stand," is simply an unfolding of that claim.

I believe that love is God's very being. If God were not love, God could both love and not love. But since God is love,

God always loves. Whatever God does, God does out of love. Which is why God's love is presuppositionless and unconditional. Since love is a relation, the One and indivisible God who is love exists as three divine persons, each both a self and an other, each both a subject and an object of love.

I believe that this God, the God who is love, creates everything that isn't God. God creates out of love and for love. Creation is a gift. Each creature and all together in their interdependence are given to each for their good and their joy. As the gift of the God of love, creation itself is good. Even marked by futility and colonized by evil, creation is still in a primordial sense good—and loved by God just for existing.

I believe that God seeks to mend all broken creatures and liberate them from futility and the power of evil. That God was in Jesus Christ. Jesus Christ was that God when he taught and healed in the land of Israel and beyond and when he was crucified for being and doing good. God "died" for God's beloved creatures even when they become God's enemies, ungodly and unjust.

I believe that this God of love seeks to dwell in each human being and in the whole creation, not as an extraneous and, perhaps, intruding add-on, but as the source of fulfillment of each unique creature. The coming of God is itself a gift which we receive by opening ourselves to God in Christ. In this way, we come to grow in being "Christs" to one another and the world. God's kind of love, situation-independent and unconditional, is therefore the hallmark of the Christian life. Love of enemy, no less than love of neighbor, is essential to Christian life. As a life of love, Christian life is often marked by suffering. Love's suffering is a *means*; Love's dance is the *goal*. That goal is a world of love, a community of creatures rightly related to God and one another. This kind of world, fully itself by being indwelled by God, is our final end.

Miroslav, your
bedraggled fellow
acolyte of Christ

JUNE 16

Dear Miroslav,

What a beautiful letter. A whole life in those words. A good life, suffered and savored to a bewildering—and therefore believable—unity.

I love the idea of after-angels, those presences we become aware of only retrospectively. "Didn't our hearts burn within us?" the disciples wonder on their way to Emmaus, *after* Jesus has revealed himself to them and vanished in the light of their understanding, which is just the plain old everyday light of life.

And in fact I have my own recent retroactive angel, and you were there. The other day when we were walking around the expensive spring-gleaming blocks north of the div school, and I was trying to tell you without really telling you why I was finding the essay I was writing on Seamus Heaney and American poetry so painful and destabilizing, you asked me, very gently (the tone changed), if I could explain why. And rather than resort to "professional" deflections, as I would usually do, I found myself (that's what it felt like, both surprising and revelatory: I *found* myself) speaking the truth. The essay had brought me face-to-face with my own work and life, the ambitions I had when I was young and the reality of my fifty-seven-year-old circumstances, and the clarity of the perception—I have fallen short—*hurt*. I wasn't sleeping well. I was picking up my own books and thumbing through them like essential instruction manuals in a language I couldn't read. I was drowning in despair. Absurdly and preposterously, yes, as the water was about an inch deep. But to an infant—and suddenly that's what I seemed to be—even a puddle can prove fatal.

We stopped on the street. And rather than offer consolation or disputing my assessment of the situation, you simply admitted to sometimes feeling the same thing. And suddenly I felt—I don't know—released. The feeling wasn't gone. The recriminations still seethed and roiled in my soul like those little blurps of air in cooking oatmeal. I still felt the cold undertow of oblivion. But I also felt lightened, alive in the spring-gleaming streets, my*self* and glad for that. Why? Nothing had changed. I can only think that the act of two bare, forked creatures acknowledging their bare, forked creatureliness enabled Christ to come among them, in them and between them. I carried the moment with me for days. I carry it now.

(And, of course, there's this: The despair was not really for my work but for my soul. It was an expression of distance from

God, a confusion to which I am apparently still prone. Poetry has its place and powers but only so long as that place and those powers remain relative to God.)

I am a Christian because of moments like that one. I am a Christian because, when I live toward God, when I allow myself (or am allowed) to inhabit a reality whose very realness depends upon God, I feel . . . right. I feel like my life and mind align with the stars and the trees, and I am both utterly myself and freed from that. It's the oldest lesson in Christianity, no? St. Paul hammers it home again and again. A certain submission to one's insignificance is the only chance of freedom. The paradox is that the "insignificance" is illusory. In God's reality—which is, simply, reality—that bare, forked creature blazes with a radiance that no lesser reality—the failures of ambition, the *achievements* of ambition—can touch.

Faith, for me, is an instinct above all else. Poetry is raveled up with this. When I allow myself to inhabit a reality whose very realness depends upon certain inevitable, immutable arrangements of language; when I *believe* in poetry, whether it's writing or reading it, then all the worldly noise that attends the art goes quiet, and in the cage of mortality I am completely free. I have given my life over to a gut feeling. It sounds to me like, for all the clarity of that credo, you have, too (that inexplicable but undeniable shift that happened in your adolescence). Theology, if it is vital, is always ex post facto: It grows out of an *experience* of God, and keeps that "bright abyss" in mind. The theology that has no such precedent, or that has forgotten it, has more to do with a syllabus than a soul.

Still, my companion bedraggler, there are too many quotation marks in that credo for me. I don't think God "died" on that hill in Judea and I don't think that in moments like the one we shared on the street we were becoming "Christs" to each other. If God didn't really die, then you need quotation marks around the resurrection as well (the supreme special effect), and if each of us was just a kind of synecdoche for Christ in that moment, then the incarnation is merely metaphor. No, I'm a fundamentalist in this sense. The utter absence of meaning in this life, the nihilistic ethos of Larkin's "Aubade" that is also a powerful and undeniable "gut feeling" I have—this was entered and undergone by God. It really is all or nothing. As is that presence on the New Haven street. I believe Christ was literally in me, and of me, in that moment, "lovely in limbs, and lovely in eyes not his," vanishing the instant I became aware.

Dostoevsky was right with his Grand Inquisitor: Religion

does everything it can to tame and control the incarnation. Why levitating saints? Because it's a strong goad to hope, first of all: We are not trapped. This implacable clock, the iron cage of cause and effect—these are of our own mind rather than reality itself. And also precisely *because* it's absurd and shocking and dramatically enacts in physical form a spiritual reality of which we are all, at some point in our lives, conscious: this split between body and soul, matter and spirit, reality and consciousness, Jesus and Christ. That the split is illusory, that we can intellectualize our way out of it, and that we are sometimes blasted out of it by some transfiguring experience in the world—this lessens, but does not altogether loosen, its hold on us.

For a carnal, contemporary conception of this split—and an instance of one of those blasting moments—check this out:

Coming

is the body's way
of weeping, after a series
of shocks is suffered, after the thrust
of things, the gist of things, becomes
apparent: the bolt is felt completely

swollen in vicinity to wrench,
the skid is clearly headed
toward an all-out insult, and the senses
one by one abandon all their stations—
into smaller hours and thinner
minutes, seconds
split—til POW—
you had it, had it coming, and it heaved, whose
    participle
wasn't heaven.
That
Was that.
And when you got
some senses back,
you asked yourself, is this
a dignified being's way
of being born? What
a thought
somebody had! (or some no-body)
out of the breathless blue, making us
double up like this, half gifted and
half robbed. 'Rise up to me,' the spirit

laughed. 'I'm
coming, I'm coming,'
the body sobbed.

—Heather McHugh

Silly, right? Sex as an intimation of the divine, bare animal rut as (almost) redemption. Yet something more serious tugs under the comic buoyancy. Sex is the closest thing many contemporary people have to a spiritual experience. It plunges them into that "split" I mention above, and occasionally makes them think—no, not "think": feel—that they've found a seam between the competing terms. Then comes the inevitable disappointment, because an experience of joy that has nowhere to go goes wrong. "Sobbed" is how the poem ends. The union—which in this instance seems singular, between one's own body and soul, one's being and Being itself—was a mirage.

But is this always true? What if the poem is more about loneliness than sex? After all, it's pretty strange to read a poem about sex in which there is no trace of another person. This could be a poem about masturbation, but for the fact that its existential intensities become, at least to this perhaps limited reader, truly absurd in that context. One could read the "failure" of the poem as a failure of love, an absence of love, at least if one thinks love really can elevate sex beyond the bestial, really can, in some sense, fuse body and soul.

Is it absurd to speak of sex in these terms? (When I was young, I found it absurd—and disturbing—for old people to speak of sex at all, but just yesterday I heard a woman on the radio lamenting that she and her husband were unable to make love after he turned *ninety*.) And here's where I have to really show my hand. When I say "love," I don't just mean love of another person. I mean the love that is "lovely in limbs, and lovely in eyes not his." The incarnation is a promise that *any* aspect of matter can be sacralized—even our most animal instances.

Or flying saints! You say that you find an ordinary human face more interesting than levitating saints. I'm sorry, my friend, but I just don't believe that. I believe that you find a face more interesting than a paragraph in a book, sure, but if on one of our walks I was suddenly jacked up into the air uttering prophecy, I'm guessing that would command your attention a bit more sharply than my lovely mug. I often hear secular people marveling at the sheer preposterousness of Christianity—God walking around the world, zapping water into wine, modern people cheerfully eating his flesh and drinking his blood—but, for me, no small part of Christianity's appeal is that very preposterousness. It is, as I said earlier, an insult to common sense, which I cherish because I am quite sure that what we call common sense is uncommonly wrong. Contemporary religion—and especially liberal Protestantism—is far too complacent in the face of this world's wonders. That it so relentlessly stresses the "extraordinary in the ordinary" is a symptom of the sickness rather than, as it purports to be, a treatment. The roots of this spiritual temerity are deep. After all, Cotton Mather, that uber Puritan, had his own experience of a levitating mystic in 1693. Several other people saw the poor woman as well and, after they helped to pull her down (they were in a house), attested to it on legal documents. Mather was wholly convinced of what he saw, and, because he associated the act with Catholics, wholly convinced it had to be the work of the Devil.

This reality we inhabit is so immense and complex, our perception of it so minute and limited. I think even Christianity is but a glimmer of the true blaze of being, but Christianity is the language I know, the language that *knows me*, and I am convinced that its truth, however limited, is a genuine key to the whole. Where does that leave me? A few years ago I wrote a poem that, at the time, seemed to me a kind of summative statement of my faith. The title is from Emily Dickinson.

No Omen but Awe

I thought it would all resolve
one day in diamond time.
Life like a gem to lift to the squint
as through a jeweler's loupe.

I thought every facet and flaw
neither facet nor flaw in some final shine;
chance and choice uncanny cognates;
form, fate.

Now I am here.
No diamond, no time, no omen but awe
that a whirlwind could in not cohering cohere.
Loss is my gift, bewilderment my bow.

("Bow" rhymes with "cow," in case there is any confusion.) Not such a rousing credo, perhaps, but it's honest. To admit the bewilderment rather than being overwhelmed by it, or trying to tie it down with theology, or even too-complacently embracing it. To make that very bewilderment into a form of obedience and praise. And these letters? They are certainly part of that "bow," that's for sure. But I also feel clearer in my confusion (that it's *mine*), stronger in my weakness (that it's Christ's), bolstered by the communion with a kindred soul. "Christ is always stronger in our brother's heart than in our own," that wise sufferer we both so admire once said. Thank you for lending me some of your strength, dear friend.

Chris

ACKNOWLEDGMENTS

I would like to thank Alice Martell, my able agent, and Stephanie Smith and Anna Calame, our attentive and efficient editors. Without them this book would not be. To Dr. Karin Fransen, my assistant, I am grateful to her for relieving me of many academic and pedagogical "chores" that would have otherwise crowded the space needed for writing, and for editorial help, especially for proofreading, as I'm a near dyslexic. From the very first day we met, Jessica Dwelle, my wife, and I have discussed the themes with which these letters are concerned. I have always admired her incisiveness and honesty in seeking the *intellectus fidei* and am grateful to have her as partner also in this important aspect of my life.

MV

I'm very grateful to my wife, Danielle Chapman, both for her direct contribution to these pages and for her clear-spirited guidance throughout. I'd also like to strongly second Miroslav's gratitude to Alice Martell, Stephanie Smith, and Anna Cálame. And finally, my research assistant Eliana Swerdlow has been involved throughout this entire process, and I have come to rely on her keen eye and poetic intuitions here as in so many other projects.

CW

NOTES

March 5

3 *"I have observed the misery":* Exodus 3:7–8.

5 *"I am who I am":* Exodus 3:14.

March 10

8 *"The eye with which I see God":* Meister Eckhart, *Selected Writings* (Penguin Classics, 1995), 179.

8 *"absolutely unmixed attention":* Simone Weil, *Gravity and Grace* (Routledge, 2002), 117.

March 16

11 *"The Word was with God":* John 1:1.

11 *"all things":* John 1:3.

11 *"some quite lunatic thought-experiment":* Denys Turner, *Thomas Aquinas: A Portrait* (Yale University Press, 2013), 120.

14 *"The heart overflows":* Martin Luther, "The Magnificat," in *Luther's Works*, ed. Jaroslav Pelikan (Concordia Publishing House, 1956), 21:300.

14 *"the bare, unfelt goodness":* Luther, "The Magnificat," 21:309.

March 20

17 *"But I need, now as then":* Robert Browning, "Rabbi Ben Ezra," Poetry Foundation, accessed August 4, 2025, https://www.poetry foundation.org/poems/43775/rabbi-ben-ezra.

18 *"One of the fatal errors":* Abraham Joshua Heschel, *God in Search of Man* (Farrar, Straus and Giroux, 1955), 8.

March 24

22 *the love of Christ:* Romans 8:38–39.

22 *"My God, my God":* Matthew 27:46.

25 *God often seems to be guarding:* Exodus 32:1–29, for instance.

March 29

34 *"the heart of obvious truths":* Anna Kamieńska, "Industrious Amazement: A Notebook," *Poetry* (March 1, 2011), https://www .poetryfoundation.org/poetrymagazine/articles/69655/industrious -amazement-a-notebook.

34 *"Nothing but grief":* Walter Brueggemann, *The Prophetic Imagination* (Fortress Press, 1978).

36 *"A thrush":* Richard Wilbur, "On Having Mis-Identified a Wildflower," *Collected Poems 1943–2004* (Harcourt, 2004), 86.

April 3

38 *"You, neighbor God":* Rainer Maria Rilke, *The Poetry of Rilke: Bilingual Edition*, trans. and ed. Edward Snow (North Point Press, 2009), 11.

38 *"I am your jug":* Rilke, *Poetry of Rilke*, 27.

40 *"You cannot help us":* Etty Hillesum, *Etty: The Letters and Diaries of Etty Hillesum, 1941–1943*, ed. Klaas A. D. Smelik, trans. Arnold J. Pomerans (William B. Eerdmans, 2002), 488.

43 *"known, shown, revealed":* Exodus 2:23–25.

44 *Septuagint in Exodus:* The Septuagint is the Greek translation of the Hebrew Bible.

44 *"groan inwardly":* Romans 8:23, 26.

April 11

45 *"We do not come to God":* Austin Farrer, *The Crown of the Year* (Dacre Press, 1952).

47 *"Only for the child does it dawn":* Rainer Maria Rilke, "Like a Holy Face," trans. by the authors.

49 *"There must be someone to live":* Etty Hillesum, *Etty: The Letters and Diaries of Etty Hillesum, 1941–1943*, ed. Klaas A. D. Smelik, trans. Arnold J. Pomerans (William B. Eerdmans, 2002), 506.

50 *"Not the round natural world":* Frederick Goddard Tuckerman, "Sonnet XXVIII," from *Sonnets, Second Series*, in *The Penguin Book of the Sonnet*, ed. Phillis Levin (Penguin, 2001), 127.

52 *"Into them [God's hands]":* Rainer Maria Rilke, *Rilke's Book of Hours: Love Poems to God*, trans. Anita Barrows and Joanna Macy (Riverhead, 1997), 98.

April 18

55 *"A 'god' is the term":* Martin Luther, *The Large Catechism* in *The Book of Concord: The Confessions of the Evangelical Lutheran Church*, eds. Robert Kolb and Timothy J. Wengert (Fortress, 2000), 386.

56 *"If your faith and trust"*: Luther, *The Large Catechism*, 386.

58 *The only poem I know:* As cited in Miroslav Volf, *I znam da sunce ne boji se tame: Teološke meditacije o Šantićevu vjerskom pjesništvu* (Izvori, 1986), 110.

April 27

65 *"After the sun's eclipse"*: Richard Wilbur, "Teresa," in *Collected Poems 1943–2004* (Harcourt, 2004), 154.

68 *"With all its eyes the animal world"*: Rainer Maria Rilke, "The Eighth Elegy" in *The Poetry of Rilke: Bilingual Edition*, trans. Edward Snow (North Point Press, 2009), 327.

69 *"Nowhere without the no"*: Snow has "Nowhere without negation," which completely loses the sonic mystery and power of the line.

May 2

76 *"transforms the value"*: William James, *The Varieties of Religious Experience*, in *William James: Writings 1902–1910*, ed. Bruce Kuklick (Library of America, 1987), 141.

76 *"The appearance of everything"*: See James, *Varieties of Religious Experience*, 229.

78 *"God has made me"*: Martin Luther, *The Small Catechism* in *The Book of Concord: The Confessions of the Evangelical Lutheran Church*, eds. Robert Kolb and Timothy J. Wengert (Fortress, 2000), 354.

80 *"outright unhealthy"*: Dietrich Bonhoeffer, *Letters and Papers from Prison*, in *Dietrich Bonhoeffer Works*, vol. 8, trans. Isabel Best et al. (Fortress, 2010), 203.

May 13

83 *"There are two atheisms":* Simone Weil, *Gravity and Grace* (Routledge, 2002), 114.

86 *"To resist the reality":* Fanny Howe, "My Father Was White but Not Quite," *Poetry Magazine*, December 1, 2008, https://www.poetryfoundation.org/poetrymagazine/articles/69163/my-father-was-white-but-not-quite.

88 *Paul said happened:* 1 Corinthians 15:15, 1 Thessalonians 1:10.

May 25

92 *"When You hide your face":* Psalm 104:29–30 in Alter, *The Hebrew Bible.*

93 *"Where can I go from Your spirit":* Psalm 139:7–12 in Alter, *The Hebrew Bible.*

95 *"Peace! Be still!":* Mark 4:39.

96 *"groaned under their slavery":* Exodus 2:23.

96 *in pain and despair:* Jan Assmann, *The Invention of Religion: Faith and Covenant in the Book of Exodus* (Princeton University Press, 2018), 118.

96 *"God heard their groaning":* Exodus 2:24–25.

97 *"My God, my God":* Psalm 22:1.

97 *"Where is your God?":* Psalm 42:3, 10.

97 *both of these Psalms:* See Mark 15:34 and John 12:27.

100 *"detachment":* Dietrich Bonhoeffer, *Letters and Papers from Prison*, in *Dietrich Bonhoeffer Works*, vol. 8, trans. Isabel Best et al. (Fortress, 2010), 359.

101 *an unpublished essay:* Sameer Yadav, "A Joban Theology of Consolation" (paper presentation, Yale Center for Faith and Culture consultation on Suffering, New Haven, CT, February 26, 2022).

103 *"If you believe":* Martin Luther, *Luther's Works*, ed. Jaroslav Pelikan (Concordia Publishing House, 1956), 31:348–49.

104 *"into the unknown":* Luther, *Luther's Works*, 25:364.

June 12

107 *"I do not understand":* John Berryman, "Eleven Addresses to the Lord," Poetry Foundation, accessed August 4, 2025, https://www.poetryfoundation.org/poems/48948/eleven-addresses-to-the-lord.

109 *"Try to remember this":* Richard Wilbur, "Walking to Sleep," in *Collected Poems 1943–2004* (Harcourt, 2004).

112 *"God would have us know":* Dietrich Bonhoeffer, *Letters and Papers from Prison*, in *Dietrich Bonhoeffer Works*, vol. 8, trans. Isabel Best et al. (Fortress, 2010), 268.

August 8

119 *I called spiritual freedom:* See Martin Hägglund, *This Life: Secular Faith and Spiritual Freedom* (Pantheon, 2019), 173–211.

120 *"the wild boar":* Psalm 80:13 (NLT).

121 *Christian way of life:* Philippians 2:6–11.

122 *"stabling under a mean roof":* John Milton, "Elegy VI," *Collected Poems and Major Prose*, ed. Merritt Y. Hughes (Hackett Publishing Company, 2003), 52.

123 *"A Christian is a perfectly free lord":* Luther, *Luther's Works*, ed. Jaroslav Pelikan (Concordia Publishing House, 1956), 31:344.

124 *"one of the most beautiful things":* Marilynne Robinson, email message to Miroslav Volf, October 16, 2020.

126 *tracing both to* ressentiment*:* Ressentiment is "a persistent, corrosive emotional pattern of resentful hatred against their enemies" on the part of those "who suffered from oppression at the hands of the noble" but who, on account of their relative powerlessness, "were denied any effective recourse against them." Nietzsche places ressentiment at the origin of all morality. R. Lanier Anderson, "Friedrich Nietzsche," in *Stanford Encyclopedia of Philosophy* (Stanford University, 1997–), published March 17, 2017, updated May 19, 2022, https://plato.stanford.edu/entries/nietzsche/.

127 *"All ancient philosophers":* Max Scheler, *Ressentiment*, trans. Lewis B. Coser and William W. Holdheim (Marquette University Press, 1998), 64.

127 *"The universe is a great chain":* Scheler, *Ressentiment*, 65.

127 *"An event that is monstrous":* Scheler, *Ressentiment*, 66.

128 *"great urge to love":* Scheler, *Ressentiment*, 67.

129 *"that he had come from God":* John 13:3–5.

August 27

135 *"Who, being in very nature God":* Philippians 2:6–8 (NIV)

137 "My *God, my God":* Matthew 27:46 and Mark 15:34.

138 *"He went up under the gray leaves":* Rainer Maria Rilke, "The Olive Garden" in *New Poems [1907]*, trans. Edward Snow, 41.

139 *"Therefore God exalted him":* Philippians 2:9–11 (NIV).

September 6

141 *"chopped up the wooden statue":* Athenagoras, "A Plea for Christians," New Advent, chapter 4, https://www.newadvent.org/fathers/0205.htm.

143 *"obedient to death":* Philippians 2:8.

143 *"the name that is above every name":* Philippians 2:9.

143 *"Let the same mind":* Philippians 2:5.

145 *"Let the little children":* Matthew 19:14.

146 *"Whoever does not take up the cross":* Matthew 10:38.

147 *"Who is Christ":* Dietrich Bonhoeffer, *Letters and Papers from Prison*, in *Dietrich Bonhoeffer Works*, vol. 8, trans. Isabel Best et al. (Fortress, 2010), 362.

147 *"experience of transcendence":* Bonhoeffer, *Letters*, 501.

148 *"ethico-social limit":* Dietrich Bonhoeffer, *Sanctorum Communio*, in *Dietrich Bonhoeffer Works*, vol. 1, trans. Reinhard Krauss and Nancy Lukens (Fortress, 2009), 51.

148 *"the world that has come of age":* Bonhoeffer, *Letters*, 451.

148 *"Come to me":* Matthew 11:28.

October 10

151 *"A god is Man's doll, you ass":* Stevie Smith, "Was He Married?," Poetry Foundation, accessed August 4, 2025, https://www.poetryfoundation.org/poems/46849/was-he-married.

153 *"Lord let me suffer much and then die":* Anna Kamieńska, "A Prayer That Will Be Answered," in *Polish Poetry of the Last Two Decades of*

Communist Rule, trans. Stanisław Barańczak and Clare Cavanagh (Northwestern University Press, 1991), 46.

155 *"MY joy, my life, my crown!":* George Herbert, "A True Hymne," George Herbert and Bemerton, accessed August 4, 2025, https://www.georgeherbert.org.uk/archives/selected_work_08.html.

158 *"No, there's no way":* James Baldwin, "Sonny's Blues," in *The Oxford Book of American Short Stories*, ed. Joyce Carol Oates (Oxford University Press, 1992), 433.

159 *"Whát I dó is me":* Gerard Manley Hopkins, "As Kingfishers Catch Fire," Poetry Foundation, accessed August 5, 2025, https://www.poetryfoundation.org/poems/44389/as-kingfishers-catch-fire.

October 24

163 *"For when we love charity":* Augustine, *The Trinity*, trans. Edmund Hill, O.P. (New City Press, 1991), 8.12.

164 *"the verse be somewhat scant":* George Herbert, "A True Hymne," George Herbert and Bemerton, accessed August 4, 2025, https://www.georgeherbert.org.uk/archives/selected_work_08.html.

164 *"which not only are":* Charles Taylor, *Sources of the Self* (Harvard University Press, 1989), 63.

164 *"love God as lice love a tramp":* Martin Luther, "The Magnificat," in *Luther's Works*, ed. Jaroslav Pelikan (Concordia Publishing House, 1956), 23:30.

165 *"de-deified, stupid, blind":* Friedrich Nietzsche, *The Joyful Science*, in *The Complete Works of Friedrich Nietzsche*, vol. 6, trans. Adrian Del Caro (Stanford University Press), §357, 230.

165 *"bird that felt itself free":* Nietzsche, *The Joyful Science*, §124, 128.

166 *"a powerful act":* Yirmiyahu Yovel, "Nietzsche and Spinoza: *amor fati* and *amor dei*," *Nietzsche as Affirmative Thinker*, ed. Yirmiyahu Yovel (Martinus Nijhoff Publishers, 1986), 200.

166 *"For God so loved the world":* John 3:16.

November 27

171 *"A serious house on serious earth":* Philip Larken, "Church Going," in *The Less Deceived: Poems* (Faber and Faber, 2012).

175 *"reaping where thou":* Matthew 25:24 (KJV).

December 24

178 *"We owe a cock to Asclepius":* Plato, *Phaedo*, in *Plato: Complete Works*, ed. John M. Cooper (Hackett, 1997), 118a.

179 *"The present form":* 1 Corinthians 7:31.

180 *"the end of a prelude to a symphony":* Abraham Joshua Heschel, "What Death Should Teach Us About Life and Living," My Jewish Learning, accessed August 4, 2025, https://www.myjewishlearning.com/article/what-death-should-teach-us-about-life-and-living/.

180 *"I am the God":* Exodus 3:6.

180 *"Now he is God":* Luke 20:38.

181 *"Every morning I am amazed":* Jürgen Moltmann, personal letter to Miroslav Volf, trans. by Volf.

181 *"In my end":* T. S. Eliot, *Four Quartets* (Harcourt, Brace & Co., 1943).

183 *"soul is more where it loves":* Bernard of Clairvaux, *On Precept and Dispensation* (Cistercian Publications, 1994), 20, 60.

183 *"hope changes the one":* Martin Luther, *Luther's Works*, ed. Jaroslav Pelikan (Concordia Publishing House, 1956), 25:364.

183 *"into the outer darkness":* Matthew 25:26–30.

183 *"Why I Am Not a Christian":* Bertrand Russell, "Why I Am Not a Christian" in *Why I Am Not a Christian and Other Essays on Religion and Related Subjects* (Touchstone, 1967).

184 *"it was not the season":* Mark 11:12–24.

189 *Paul said of his own sermons:* See 1 Corinthians 2:1–8.

189 *philosophical treatise:* Nicholas Wolterstorff, *Divine Discourse: Philosophical Reflections on the Claim That God Speaks* (Cambridge University Press, 1995).

189 *"like unto" the first:* Matthew 22:39 (KJV).

190 *"Whoever comes to me":* Luke 14:26.

190 *"throughout the camp":* Exodus 32:27.

190 *"This is my body":* Matthew 26:26, Mark 14:22, Luke 22:19.

January 19

194 *"One thing does not exist":* Jorge Luis Borges, "Everness," in *Collected Poems 1943–2004*, trans. Richard Wilbur (Harcourt, 2006), 242.

198 *"I think there is no light":* George Oppen, "The Poem," in *New Collected Poems* (New Directions, 2008), 309.

198 *"It's when I read":* Darcey Steinke and Rick Moody, eds., *Joyful Noise: The New Testament Revisited* (Back Bay Books, 1999).

February 29

202 *"God saves the metal":* Jorge Luis Borges, "Everness," in *Collected Poems 1943–2004*, trans. Richard Wilbur (Harcourt, 2006), 242.

203 *"He must increase":* John 3:30.

204 *"one believes":* Romans 10:10.

204 *"God is love":* 1 John 4:8, 16.

205 *"the raging, boundless sea":* Arthur Schopenhauer, *The World as Will and Representation*, trans. Judith Norman et al. (Cambridge University Press, 2014), 1: 375; Friedrich Nietzsche, *The Joyful Science*, in *The Complete Works of Friedrich Nietzsche*, vol. 6, trans. Adrian Del Caro (Stanford University Press), §124, 128.

205 *"have no faith":* Mark 4:35–40.

April 17

206 *Jack Miles's "biography" of God:* Jack Miles, *God: A Biography* (Vintage Books, 1996).

210 *"I shall set my law":* Jeremiah 31:33–34 (REB).

June 2

214 *"be at home in our time":* Abraham Joshua Heschel, "On Prayer," Open Siddur Project, August 10, 2018, https://opensiddur.org/miscellanea/pedagogy/on-prayer-by-abraham-joshua-heschel-1969.

216 *"hidden powers inherent":* Carlos Eire, *They Flew: A History of the Impossible* (Yale University Press, 2023), 266.

217 *"that the Lord was about to":* Eire, *They Flew*, 74.

217 *"There is little to be gained":* Jack Miles, *God: A Biography* (Vintage Books, 1996), 13.

218 *"One of the very earliest statements":* Miles, *God*, 14.

218 *"visiting the iniquity":* Exodus 34:7.

218 *"a child shall not suffer":* Ezekiel 18:20.

219 *"For those in whom the will":* Arthur Schopenhauer, *The World as Will and Representation*, trans. Judith Norman et al. (Cambridge University Press, 2014), I: 439.

219 *"a wind from God swept over":* Genesis 1:2.

220 *"every inclination of the thoughts":* Genesis 6:5.

221 *"The Lord said in his heart":* Genesis 8:21.

222 *"God has decided to remain faithful":* Shai Held, *Judaism Is About Love: Recovering the Heart of Jewish Life* (Farrar, Straus and Giroux, 2024), 378.

222 "I believe *that love is God's very being":* Adapted from Miroslav Volf, *Exclusion and Embrace* (Abingdon, 2019), 307–9.

June 16

229 *"is the body's way":* Heather McHugh, "Coming," in *Hinge and Sign* (Wesleyan University Press, 1994), 15.

234 *"I thought it would all resolve":* Christian Wiman, "No Omen but Awe," *Plough*, November 30, 2021, https://www.plough.com/en/topics/culture/poetry/poem-no-omen-but-awe.

235 *"Christ is always stronger":* Dietrich Bonhoeffer, *Life Together*, trans. John W. Doberstein (SCM Press, 1965), 12.

CREDITS AND PERMISSIONS

Grateful acknowledgment is given to the following for the use of their work in this publication:

"On Having Mis-Identified a Wild Flower" by Richard Wilbur on p. 36 from *Collected Poems 1943–2004* by Richard Wilbur. Copyright © 2004 by Richard Wilbur. Used by permission of HarperCollins Publishers.

Excerpts on p. 38–39, 68–69 from *The Poetry of Rilke: Bilingual Edition* by Rainer Maria Rilke, translated and edited by Edward Snow. Translation © 2009 by Edward Snow. Reprinted by permission of North Point Press, Farrar, Straus and Giroux. All Rights Reserved.

"Teresa" by Richard Wilbur on p. 65–66 from *The Mind Reader* by Richard Wilbur. Copyright © 1955, 1966, 1969, 1970, 1971, 1972, 1973, 1974, 1975, 1976 by Richard Wilbur. Used by permission of HarperCollins Publishers.

"The Olive Garden" by Rainer Maria Rilke on p. 138–39 from *New Poems [1907]* by Rainer Maria Rilke, a bilingual edition translated by Edward Snow. Translation copyright © 1984 by Edward Snow. Reprinted by permission of North Point Press, a division of Farrar, Straus and Giroux. All Rights Reserved.

"Was He Married?" on p. 151–52 from *Collected Poems of Stevie Smith*, copyright ©1972 by Stevie Smith. Reprinted by permission of New Directions Publishing Corp./Faber and Faber Ltd.

"A Prayer That Will Be Answered" by Anna Kamieńska on p. 153–54, from *Polish Poetry of the Last Two Decades of Communist Rule: Spoiling Cannibals Fun*, translated by Stanislaw Baranczak and Clare Cavanagh. Evanston: Northwestern University Press, 1991. Copyright © 1991 by Northwestern University Press. Published 1991. All rights reserved.

Extract from "Church Going" by Philip Larkin on p. 171 from *The Complete Poems of Philip Larkin* by Philip Larkin, edited by Archie Burnett. Copyright © 2012 by The Estate of Philip Larkin. Introduction copyright © 2012 by Archie Burnett. Reprinted by permission of Farrar, Straus and Giroux. All Rights Reserved/Faber and Faber Ltd.

Extract from "Everness" by Jorge Luis Borges, translated by Richard Wilbur, on p. 194, from *Collected Poems 1943–2004* by Richard Wilbur. Copyright © 2004 by Richard Wilbur. Used by permission of HarperCollins Publishers.

"The Poem" by George Oppen on p. 198, from *New Collected Poems of George Oppen*, copyright ©1981 by George Oppen. Reprinted by permission of New Directions Publishing Corp./Carcanet Press.

"Coming" by Heather McHugh on p. 229–31, from *Hinge & Sign: Poems 1968–1993*, copyright © 1994 by Heather McHugh. Published by Wesleyan University Press. Used by permission.

"No Omen but Awe" by Christian Wiman on p. 234 from *Zero at the Bone: Fifty Entries Against Despair* by Christian Wiman. New York: Farrar, Straus and Giroux: 2023. Used by permission.

MIROSLAV VOLF is the Henry B. Wright Professor of Theology at Yale Divinity School and the founding director of the Yale Center for Faith and Culture. His books include *Exclusion and Embrace*, winner of the Grawemeyer Award in Religion, and *Life Worth Living*, a *New York Times* bestseller.

CHRISTIAN WIMAN is the Clement-Muehl Professor of the Arts at Yale Divinity School. He is the author, editor, or translator of fifteen books, including *Zero at the Bone* and *Hammer Is the Prayer*. His work appears regularly in *Harper's*, *The New Yorker*, and *Commonweal*.